Hypnosis De-Mystified: Imagine That!

Walt McCoy, PhD.

D1444613

2
ISBN: 9781481263092

Acknowledgments

Hypnotherapists are a very gregarious lot. They love to get together at conventions, workshops, classes, and seminars, to share insights and techniques. I have rarely sensed the competitiveness that interferes with the free sharing of experiences and anecdotes that is characteristic of them. As do all true professionals, they take pride and joy in their work. Hypnosis is a truly collaborative field. Science is supposed to work like this:

Researchers publish papers that describe in detail what they did and what they found out. They also are expected to provide a review of prior research on the topic. This so that other researchers can repeat; or replicate, the study to see if they get the same results, a method of verification. But here is what tends to happen in the hallowed halls of academia. The scientists focus upon their own line of research, and leave the reading, summarizing, and reporting of other related research to their graduate students. They don't really communicate with each other, so that the knowledge is not really cumulative and progressive, but dispersed and fragmented.

Replication and verification rarely happen, because it is not readily publishable in a "publish or perish" academic world.

"The host of specialists narrow their field and dig down

deeper and deeper until they can't see each other from hole to hole. But the treasure their toil brings to light, they place on the ground above. A different kind of specialist should be sitting there...and piece all the different facts together."

Thor Heyerdahl

Most of this book is original with myself, but much of it has been inspired by conversations with my colleagues. I frankly don't remember the difference. Whenever I remember someone who influenced me in a specific topic, I will cite them. I will place a bibliography of those authors and teachers who have inspired me at the end; I apologize to those who I may have innocently forgotten.

You know who you are.

I would like to dedicate this book to Milton Erickson, M.D., who is perhaps our greatest pioneer in hypnosis and such. You can get his amazing videos from the Erickson Foundation in Phoenix, or at a university library.

5
Table of Contents

Introduction   pp 9

Chapter I. FAQs   pp 14

There are many myths and misconceptions about hypnosis. This is your chance to be informed accurately. If you don't find the answer to your question here, you can contact me on my website and I'll reply with your answer.

Chapter II. A Theoretical Model of Mind.

pp 30

Understanding about the mind does not really require years of study. This chapter offers a model that makes understanding hypnosis readily accessible. It's also easy to read.

Chapter III. An example of a Hypnosis Script

pp 53

I use this induction script very often, especially with groups. It will introduce you to relaxation guided imagery, and if you try it out with someone (yourself?), you will begin to get comfortable with hypnosis.

Chapter IV. Hypnosis and Medicine.   pp 68

Modern medicine knows that mind and body are actually one and the same. They need to be in cooperation to optimize healing. There is really no medical condition that cannot respond to hypnosis. The Mind is a very powerful thing.

Chapter V. Sports and Performance Hypnosis   pp 89

You can gain more control over all of your abilities and all of your skills. Get in the "zone" and maximize your athletic performance, and also your job performance.

Chapter VI. Fun with Puns, duble meanings, and cunfusion.   pp 109

There is an unusual language that the unconscious parts of your mind understand very well. Many Hypnotherapists use that odd way of speaking to enhance communication with those parts.

Chapter VII. Identity and the Dumb Blond Syndrome: The Metaphor Approach   pp 120

We build our sense of self from our role models, and from the many different roles we play every day with other people. Some of them could use some adjusting.

Chapter VIII. Illustrative Cases and Approaches.   pp 133

Here are many of my actual cases, and how I dealt with them. (Disguised, of course.) This might be my favorite chapter.

Chapter IX. Using Your Mind For a Change?
pp 194

In this one we discover the dynamics and requirements for that rare phenomenon of changing one's mind. Only you and I are able to do that, and I'm not so sure about you.

Chapter X. Guided Imagery in Persuasion, Parenting, Sales, Education, and Romance   pp 206

We try to do these things almost every day. Why not sharpen your skills in them?

Appendix I Choosing a Hypnotherapist

pp 250

Appendix II The Therapeutic Relationship

pp 253

Appendix III A Bibliography, For Those That Like This
Topic

pp 25

Introduction- Read This!

Many people are afraid of hypnosis. The very word recalls old images of evil magicians with spiral eyes who turn people into zombies, for nefarious and unspeakable reasons. Even many therapists are nervous about it. I think they are because they either fear failure, or they dread the intense focus that it requires. Some even wonder if it might be unsafe, or fraudulent.

That is why I have reserved the first chapter to answer FAQ's, and to tell the truth about what hypnosis is, how it works, and what it is not. Later, I will share many stories about my clients. (disguised, of course). I'll also offer scripts, that I have found to be effective and worthwhile.

I have learned a lot about hypnosis, and I know things that other's don't yet know.

It comes to me now, near the end of my time, that many of our learning's are lost. Perhaps, maybe we can speak longer. As a young guy, I learned how to do some things. Like run, jump, peddle a bike, whittle, and camp out.

Later, I learned how to contemplate.

And that is what this book is all about.

It is intended for those who might want to experience hypnosis, for therapists who may want to add hypnosis to their toolbox, and for those who are curious.

Please read it slowly. Take enough time to contemplate. Don't rush. There is time for contemplation and reflection. If you feel like you have had enough for a while, obey that instinct.

I made a commitment to become a psychotherapist when my mom was in a mental hospital. When I visited her there, she tried very hard to be cheery; and she showed me the places, people, things, and rules that ran the darned place. The word I thought of was "medieval". After I graduated, I worked for a while at the place. That's where I met the group of psychiatrists that later hired me. More about that later.

I was a classically trained therapist, and I had just a few methods of therapy that I was trained to use. Much of my early career I spent seeking out and learning other types of therapy, looking for ways to become more effective, because I wasn't fully satisfied with my results. They took too long, and often didn't work all that well.

I once published a paper that identified 130 different kinds of psychotherapy, along with the evaluation research that gauged their effectiveness. There are some that are very close to a waste of time.

Often, there are fads that run through the whole therapy community, whenever someone thinks of a flashy new label and writes a book. Most of those pass on by.

Later into my career I discovered Stress Management, with all its many techniques, and I got myself certified in that. It became most of what I did- I began to see the vast majority of symptoms as resulting from stress. Later, this logically led to Guided Imagery and to Hypnosis. So I started to spend my yearly continuing education budget going to seminars and workshops in hypnosis. At my third one, the moderator actually made us pair off and do some guided imagery with each other. It was like a whole new universe of understanding for me, and I was hooked. I never looked back.

Most people call it hypnosis. But I think that the word is much too pretentious, and maybe even scary. Whatever it is that we do, when we do that, is so much more fun and growing, that I struggle for a word. "Guided imagery" is pretty good. Some call it neurolinguistics. One of my clients called it "day-dreaming together", and that is really very accurate! You could also call it "guided abstract reasoning". Bill O'Hanlon calls it "Possibility Land". I'd bet; when you finish this book, that you will have thought of a better word.

You can do hypnosis- it's very do-able. And when you will do it well, it is easy.

Trust me on that, at least for now.

Regarding style: I have written this book to be accessible to a popular audience of the curious. In the hallowed halls of academia, scientific writing requires a very rigid, stuffy, formal style. That's why nobody actually reads it. When was the last time you read a scientific research article in a professional journal? Scientific journals are mostly used to decorate coffee tables in waiting rooms. Students learn to merely read the short summary at the top, which is called the abstract. It will get you through the exam.

The first requirement of a scientific research report, is a detailed review of all previous research in the topic. Not even researchers actually read this stuff. They make their graduate students do it. In scientific publications, you are not allowed to do any reasoning; you cannot say anything without citing all of the research behind what you say. Very boring! Graham Hancock, Leon Festinger, and Michael Cremo have written extensively on this problem.

That is why I have included very few sources in this book. I have already done the scientific research review, and I won't lie to you. If you want to investigate some idea further, it is much easier for you to do a keyword search on your computer, rather than being forced to read about it in this book. That would spoil the fun for us.

I have placed a selected bibliography of sources at the end.

I have also tried to keep it short. That is because I would like you not to feel rushed, and to feel that you can read at a leisurely pace. Let's not make it into work, in order to merely finish the book. There are some ideas; I hope, that are worth a pause, and contemplation.

They tell me to write about what I know. So here goes.

Go, now, on this journey of joyous discovery, and my voice will go with you.

Chapter I

FAQs

Q. What Is hypnosis?

A. Wow! You really cut to the quick. The short answer is that "hypnosis" occurs whenever one focuses his/her attention away from the "here and now" of reality, into the world of abstract reasoning and imagery, or Imagination. The land of possibilities.

As an example: most people have had the experience of driving alone at night, and suddenly to realize that you have no memory of the last 20 miles, or the last 20 minutes.

(Don't let that frighten you, research shows that your reaction time to any unexpected incident is actually faster while in that state of mind; probably because your unconscious minds don't need to wait for your conscious mind to make a decision; they know what to do already.) What happened was that one of your unconscious minds wanted to dream about a problem, and tried to understand it better, or at least differently. (If "minds" sounds unusual to you, don't worry. We'll talk more about that later.) So while you were bored, it went to work .You were entranced, or at least in a very thoughtful mood.

Another example might be movies. If you don't trance out at a movie, and forget that it is fiction, and respond emotionally to it as if it were real; then you probably won't recommend it to a friend.

In show business, they call that the "willing suspension of disbelief". The only difference between movies and hypnosis, is that movies give you the imagery. In books and in hypnosis, you make your own imagery, just as you like it.

Driving in a trance is really quite a deep "trance" (call it maybe "alternative state of awareness)"- Deep enough to shut out pain!

Some hypnosis can also be achieved without entrancement. Picture this:

One of my students came into my office, and was upset about his grade on an essay. He had clearly decided to be assertive, perhaps intimidating, even angry.

My first impulse was to respond in the same way, and show that I was also good at assertiveness and anger; which would have turned it into a contest of wills. In fact, I knew I could win that one, because I had the grade book! Gotcha!

Do you think we could have resolved the problem in that mode?

I let him vent out, and as he paused, I said

"Let me stop-, and think- and see if I can understand what you're saying. Can you put that in different words?"

His eyes widened and his jaw dropped for a couple of beats, and then he gave a good rational explanation of what he was trying to say on his essay. He actually intended some good points on the essay, but under time pressure, he didn't express them clearly.

<u>Now-we could find ways to resolve it.</u>

Look back at what happened here. I said "Let me stop...". Here I am expressing a willingness to be calm.,...and think". Here I am modeling reasonableness. "and see", thoughtfulness. "if I can understand", willingness to listen", "Can you put that in different words?" Let's go over that.

He really had no choice but to reflect the above strategies that I told him I was doing. Otherwise he'd have looked like a jerk, even in his own eyes. We did reach a resolution.

Here is a golden secret about persuasion:

People have a strong tendency to reflect whatever of their emotional and intellectual resources that you are using at the time. If you want them to reflect specific state of mind, just do it first, and they will follow willingly.

That is precisely how President Reagan won the debates with President Carter. Reagan knew how to get the audience to walk along beside him.

You could say that hypnosis is daydreaming about alternatives, and you'd be right.

Q. Do you have to lose consciousness' or be asleep, with hypnosis?

A. No. As a matter of fact, most people report sharper awareness during hypnosis. They report that they remember noises, events, or overheard conversations that they usually just tune out. Their other minds are alert, and not drowned out by their first mind.

Q. Is hypnosis dangerous?

A. It can be misused. (like anything else). For example, we always consult with a person's physician before doing pain management. We don't want to cover up pain, while recognizing that pain is important to medical diagnosis and treatment.

There are rumors that some law enforcement or intelligence agencies have tried to use hypnosis or drugs to control people.

(I can't think of a way to do that. It really can't be done. It is entirely voluntary. Nor would I try... What are we without our ethics?)

Q. Can anyone be hypnotized?

A. There are exceptions. I need to explain.

First, technically speaking, no one can "be hypnotized." It is not something the hypnotherapist does, it is something the client does. The hypnotist merely provides instructions about how to do it ("Imagine, if you will...") If someone doesn't want to do it, they simply won't do it.

Second, one needs normal verbal skills, in order to understand the instructions.

Third, a normal ability to control one's mind(s) is necessary. People with severe psychoses, or who are under the influence of substances, can't do it.

As I think about it, I remember an exception to what I just said. I had a client who didn't believe in hypnosis, and didn't want to try it. He was in my office for pain management, which his insurance company insisted that he submit to.

One of the things I do with pain clients is to ask them, on a scale of one to ten, how much it hurts. They might say "9". Then I ask how much it bothers them. They might say "8".I ask again at the end of the session, and it almost always goes down to maybe "8" and "6". Just a way to gauge progress and to demonstrate that we haven't wasted our time. So this client answered those questions as we began. But when I began trance induction he just reached over, grabbed a book from the bookcase, and began reading!

I knew that when a person's first mind is distracted or otherwise engaged, the other minds are free to listen in on whatever is going on. The first mind usually makes too much noise for the others to stay involved. So I just went on with the session. He was already in a trance!

I could tell by the subtle changes in his skin color and in the tonus of some of his facial muscles that something was changing.

I do not see this as doing something against his will. Almost all of your minds are on your side, and they will look out for you, even if you think you disagree with them.

So we had a successful session, and we went on in the same way for, I think, about 5 or 6 more sessions. He got down to "5" and "3", which was tolerable pain enough to return to work. He came back a few months later for a refresher tune-up.

Q. You say "almost all" of our minds are on our side. Aren't the ones who are not on our side dangerous?

A. We have at least one mind that wants us to atone for our

sins by punishing us. It usually punishes us with shame and guilt, and that's one of the things that make us human. A sense of guilt is often called "conscience", and we surely want to keep that, because it guides moral and ethical behavior. But sometimes it can become strong enough to actually cause us to have accidents, for example. At the extreme, it can turn into unconscious suicidal impulses. That's usually what makes people terrified of heights.

Some people, during the years of the "Black Plague" in the middle ages, became convinced that the pandemic spread of the disease was caused by Divine retribution for the sins of mankind. Many began to find very gruesome ways to punish their bodies, and many died from the resultant wounds. In spite of being a dramatic demonstration of Faith, it didn't work.

In some places, this "atonement" trance behavior continues to this day.

When this happens, the symptoms are actually a trance in themselves. In that case, we change our methods to get the person OUT of a counter-productive trance. For example, we might work on strengthening the mind that's in charge of self-esteem.

Q. My religion prohibits "conjuring". I think it's somewhere in Leviticus.

A. The word "conjuring" actually means, the calling forth of demons. The closest I have ever come to that, is asking someone's disagreeable spouse to become involved in therapy.

There is nothing magical or supernatural in hypnosis.

If it is seen as a difficulty, one thing that we can do is invite the appropriate clergy to sit in and keep an eye on us. I sometimes suspect that some of them want to keep us under their control.

Q. What if someone doesn't come out of hypnosis?

A. In no way does hypnosis detract from your control of yourself. It's fundamental purpose is to strengthen your own control! To stop doing hypnosis, is just as easy as taking a deep breath, maybe easier.

We often "count down" a client. It goes like this: (slowly)

"I'm going to slowly count backwards from 5 to 1. As I count, you will be able to comfortably return to the here and now, very easily and without effort.

Counting now from 5, and down to 4. Notice that you can control going up, and control going down. (a little confusion doesn't hurt). Now 3. Wiggle your toes.. Notice the new energy in your toes. (toes often flex during orgasm) Now 2. Notice how relaxed and refreshed you feel, - (pause) as you recognize that your abilities belong to you, and you can use them whenever you wish. Annnd- one."

(Wait for them to stretch and smile).

"Take a few moments to get your bearings".

We do this not because the client can't do it by themselves. We do it because a trance is a very enjoyable, refreshing experience, and the client might wish to stay there a little longer. To suddenly ask them to stop can be jarring, and even annoying to them. So we give plenty of warning and try to make it more comfortable.

One interesting case comes to mind. I made a house call to a teenage girl's home, because her parents were panicking because she frequently disobeyed them; she had stayed out most of the night. The girl was good at hypnosis, so it was OK if the parents sat in on our session. After exploring her defiance some more, (the parents were clearly tranced out also), I counted her out. She didn't wake up, she just laid there. The parents were very upset, thinking she might be like that forever! "What should we do!?"

I let them know that she was probably very tired and was just taking a nap. She will wake up by the time we finish a cup of coffee. And of course she did.

Q. It seems to me that behavior and abilities must provide some survival value, or they wouldn't exist. What evolutionary survival value does hypnosis have?

A. I'm glad you brought that up., it's an interesting topic.

I have defined a "trance" as occurring anytime one's attention is not focused on the here and now of reality, but is focused on abstract ideas, other places or times, or problems. In other words, daydreaming. I have also defined hypnosis as "daydreaming together". I really can't think of a reliable difference between daydreaming and night dreaming, except that night dreaming tends to be preceded by sleep waves in the brain.

Dreaming is essential to rational thought. It is during dreaming that our minds communicate and agree to cooperate. It is a necessary problem solving ability.

The language of our first mind, which is words, is simply too slow and awkward to deal with the complexity of life. The main task of our first mind is to form words and communicate our logic with others.

Think about what your other minds are capable of!
They:

1. regulate your heart, digestion and metabolism,, and blood and brain chemistry.

2. fight disease.

3. assume the duty of breathing, whenever you're not paying attention to it.

4. blink, cough and sneeze, or remove your hand from a

hot stove.

5. control balance, coordination, process information from our senses, and carry on goal-directed muscle activity.

It would be impossible for our first mind to carry on all these hyper-complex activities in verbal mode. Just too slow, awkward, and imprecise. Our bodies run on analog information, not digital information.

Imagine trying to ride a bicycle if you had to think; in words, about fine tuning each of the hundreds of muscles you have in your body, maintain balance and a sense of destination, while simultaneously thinking about your job and listening to Rush Limbaugh on the headphones. It won't work!

Because of taking over these jobs, our other minds have made it possible for selective evolution (or God, if you wish) to develop our first mind, which has rational logic and the ability to dream (day or night). With dreaming, we can consider possibilities and make plans. That ability brought us to the top of the food chain.

Not only that, but daydreaming about sex tends to increase our reproductive potential.

Q. Do people remember hypnosis sessions?

A. Yes, and they remember much more detail than

otherwise. That's because our first mind (when fully active) filters out events and sensory information that it feels is not important at the time. It is able to ignore stuff.

In hypnosis, our other minds record everything. That's why people can often recall events with hypnosis, which they otherwise have forgotten.

They tell me that hypnotists can cause one to not remember the content of an hypnotic session, by using post-hypnotic suggestion. I suspect that's true, but I have never tried it. I haven't tried it, simply because I see no productive reason for it. (except maybe in stage/entertainment hypnosis, just for fun). You might go to the back of the book, and read the appendix on "The Therapeutic Relationship".

I always wanted my clients to remember everything, and to tell their friends!

Q. Can hypnosis create false memories?

A. Yes. Repeated trips into fantasy can alter our memory of real events. It's like when friends get together and reminisce about past times. At high school reunions, the stories get better with each telling, and our memories of the real events become different, exaggerated, and even fantastic. Have you ever seen a convention of flying saucer abductees? They sometimes unwittingly adopt other people's memories. Memories are negotiable.

But it does not require hypnosis to change memories. When witnesses to accidents or crimes have a chance to discuss together what they saw, their stories change, rather dramatically. And they are abashed when the change of story is pointed out to them; they were not aware of the change.

It has been shown that police can influence witnesses in a line-up, by giving subtle, maybe unconscious clues about their own opinion. There are documented cases where social workers have instilled a false memory of sexual abuse. It is human nature to readily take on a "victim" role. Being a victim has some nice social advantages. Even little children discover that they get more attention, concern, and care when they are sick. This is called "secondary gain". Health professionals are specifically trained to deal with secondary gain, because it can actually interfere with physical healing! They now make you get up and walk, very soon after surgery. (As in all professions, there are always some who will take improper advantage of such things. Signs of greed are a warning signal.).

You can very clearly see the "victim" role when a TV announcer interviews a victim of a crime or accident. Hitler persuaded the German people that they were poor because they were victims of Jewish bankers. People actually started having memories of bad experiences with Jews!

It is highly unethical, maybe even actionable, for a hypnotist to do this deliberately. And it is incompetent to do it inadvertently.

Q. Can someone be seduced under hypnosis?

A. Not unless they want to be.

Q. My hypnotherapist sometimes says things that seem nonsensical or absurd to me. Is that my fault or his?

A. It may not be a fault at all. Hypnotherapists try to develop the skill of speaking in the strange language of the unconscious minds. There, the strict rules of logic and it's communication don't need to be enforced.

Often, in working with golfers (is that an oxymoron?) I might suggest: "... so that you can try easier, rather than harder". That makes perfect sense down there.

If it intrudes and disrupts your focus, just tell him. He will either stop it, or guide you to a deeper trance.

Q. What does it feel like to be in hypnosis?

A. You will probably not experience anything unusual, until afterwards. There is no identified hypnotic feeling except maybe a sense of distance or detachment. Many people insist that they were not in hypnosis at all, except that now their pain is better, for example. Just about everyone reports that it was pleasant, relaxing, and refreshing. Distressed or anxious feelings are almost non-existent. Let me give you an exception to that rule, as an example.

As an inexperienced student of hypnosis, I once went through a progressive relaxation routine (that I had just learned) with a friend. She was a close friend, so she had some trust in me.

After a simple induction, we went (daydreaming) to a beach in the Caribbean. We experienced the sun on our skin, the warmth of the sand, drifting clouds, the sounds of gulls, the rhythm of the waves- all the rich sensations.

I asked her to imagine that she were an inflatable doll, with an inflatable nozzle on her toe. We opened the nozzle, and she slowly deflated (limb by limb). Then a wave washed up and gently lifted her feet, then slowly receded and rested her feet on the sand again. We did this with each limb. Until she gently washed out on the water, and rolled with the swells.

At this point she jumped up, and glared at me , with anger in her eyes, as if I had inexcusably betrayed a sacred trust! Turned out she couldn't swim, and was afraid of the water.

Live and learn.

Q. How should I prepare for a hypnotic session?

A. Nothing is required, except sobriety. Wear comfortable clothes. Let your hypnotherapist take it from there. Expect to chat for some time in order to begin knowing each other. (see the story just above).

Q. You keep talking about "other minds", in the plural. That's new to me, and I would like to discuss it

A. That's the topic of our next chapter.

Chapter II

A Theoretical Model of Mind

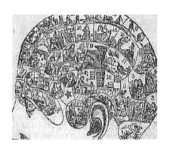

Part 1- Background.

Let me digress about theoretical Psychology, just so that we are all on the same page.

Sigmund Freud (1856-1939) has been justly called the father of modern theoretical and clinical Psychology. He was a Physician who developed a model of mind functioning and of "neurosis" (a term no longer used), and a method of treating such, called Psycho-analysis. His prolific essays, containing "case studies" were the basis of almost cult-like popularity. His legacy and methods are still popular today. Moving from Vienna to the U.S. to escape the rise of Nazism, and to seek treatment for throat cancer (he was a chain cigar smoker), he became world famous. I spent a lot of time as a student studying Freud.

Perhaps his most lasting contributions are his concepts of the unconscious mind, and his model of mind functioning. Others, before Freud, had discovered how to use the unconscious; they just didn't have a name for it.

For example; Diogenes, the Greek historian, wrote about a philosopher who composed philosophical treatises while "sleep walking". Some of Schubert's melodies came to him in dreams, and those seem to have been his favorites. Voltaire and Tartini had the same experience. Condorecet, the French mathematician, dreamed his way into solving formulas.

Sir Walter Scott, when faced with "writer's block", would often just go to bed.

He often discovered in the morning that he had dreamed of an idea, and then would continue writing. Schopenhauer once said that "My will is asleep when I do my most effective thinking, which is usually in a semi-trance". Descartes, Leibnitz, Milton, and Rossini would stimulate their own creativity by meditating (hiding?) under piles of blankets.

You might have done that at some time, also? I have.

Coleridge would sometimes fall asleep at his desk, and wake up to find that he had composed several hundred lines of verse. He said that he composed the entire "Kubla Khan" in a trance. Einstein said that "The only really valuable thing is intuition". Beethoven composed the entire Divine Ninth, while totally deaf, and within his own mind!

MLK said- "I have a dream."

Freud postulated just 3 minds; he called them as id, ego, and superego. Very briefly, the id is in charge of "wanting". It can want anything and/or everything. It is "polymorphous perverse," it has desires and impulses, many of which we are not aware. (because they may be naughty- those impulses may then become "repressed".) Impulses or wants, both conscious and unconscious, are carefully watched by the superego, which contains (hopefully) a code of ethics and morality, derived from our role models.

The superego dives a thumbs up or thumbs down to our impulses. Remember they we are probably not aware that this is going on, all the time.

If we do it (or think about it) anyway, it can punish us, with shame and guilt. If we keep it up, it can cause emotional or even physical illness. If it's OK with the superego, it is passed to the ego.

The ego is the one that thinks, and uses conscious logic and words. The ego is the rational mind that we can exercise limited control of. Its job is to come up with a good plan for getting what we want. Freud saw "neurosis" symptoms as signaling extreme conflict among these 3 minds. As Red Skelton said, "If I dood id, it be bad."

It should be stressed that these "minds" should not be viewed as actual parts of the brain. You can't find them with a n MRI scan. They are simply related clusters of functions, or abilities. You could call them metaphors, or analogies. We behave "as if" they actually existed.

I remember in graduate school there was a comedy scientific journal called the "Worm Runner's Digest". It was published with a serious journal about Developmental Psychobiology. (Read as "animal brains"). To read the Worm Runners Digest, you simple turned it backwards and upside down, and turned the pages left to right.

Anyway, there was one tongue-in-cheek article about rat brains. The authors were ablating rats (sucking out parts of the brains with a vacuum tube) just to see what would happen. So one group of rats demonstrated frenzied and continuous reproductive behavior. Their conclusion was that they had ablated the rats' superegos.

I can't resist a word of caution to parents. Children are born with ids. They are naturally good at wanting stuff. The ego (thinker), ant the superego (judge), take some time to develop. The brain is not capable of carrying out these functions until after a process of neurological and social development. That is why trying to explain things to pre-schooler's is pretty much a waste of time. It also annoys both of you. It's much like trying to discuss Hamlet with a Great Dane. They can learn a lot of words, but they don't really use them to think with yet. And the development of the superego may not be complete until the mid teens. That's why they often forget to obey as soon as you are out of sight.

But today Psychoanalysis is nearly extinct, as are its practitioners. It has always been limited to the wealthy, not only because of very large fees for nearly daily sessions, but because it has explicit and measurable goals and no defined end point. Effectiveness can only be measured by client satisfaction and return; there is virtually no measurable symptom improvement. I became disillusioned and impatient with it early on in my career.

The psychoanalytic model is too simple to reflect the human psyche. The infinite complexity of human individuals requires a potentially infinite model . We can do so much more, than jus merely want, and judge, and plan.

Freud; himself, was forced to write as an apologist for Psychoanalysis, for the reasons I mentioned.

He advocated many other forms of treatment, including injected cocaine and "Mesmerism". (Franz Mesner, 1734-1815, is credited with discovering hypnosis. But he thought that the phenomenon was the result of "animal magnetism" and other spiritual and supernatural powers. In other words magic). Freud was enthralled with it, but his writings reveal that he misunderstood or did not understand it. His methods of Mesmerism seem hopelessly primitive today, and he eventually gave up on it. But he didn't give up cocaine, because he and his patients were addicted to it. You see, Freud was trained as a research physician, rather than as a practicing clinical physician.

He has been called a "pan-sexualist", because he maintained dogmatically that sex was the root of all human motives. His own inner circle of theorists balked at this assertion, and he dismissed some of them. He also dismissed female rancor as "penis envy".

I am reminded of the old country/western song concerning what it's all about, titled "Faster Horses, Older Whiskey, Younger Women, More Money". By this measure, Freud would appear to have gotten one out of 4. I suppose batting . 250 is pretty good for a pitcher. But now we know that there are any number of human motives and values, and they are all moving parts. Focusing on just one of them as the root of it all, actually leads us away from a full appreciation of reality.

But back to the point, Freud deserves his place in history. His work in unconscious processes was a genuine breakthrough. However, it's time to move on.

Let me work up to a more adequate model by offering my first introduction to "glove anesthesia". The meaning of that term will become clear. I was at a weeklong hypnosis seminar hosted by Don Aspromonte. We had a medical student in the class who was having academic problems because he kept falling asleep while trying to study. Now-other methods of psychotherapy would require a long process of diagnosis, treatment planning, team meetings, assigning of a primary therapist, and likely months of treatment!

But Don took him/us on a trip. I'm going to summarize it, in order to save time and pages.

After a quick hypnotic induction (for example, the one in our next chapter), we were on a mountain snow-packed trail (we were in Denver at the time). We could hear the crunch of the snow as we walked. There was a large log home up ahead, and we decided to explore it. Walking across the echoing porch and opening the squeaking door, (property rights don't exist in dreams, and med students tend to become adept in listening/hearing mode) we saw a cheery blaze in the fireplace. We warm ourselves. We explored the halls and rooms. (The unconscious recognizes that a home is a metaphor/symbol for the self, and exploring a home provides a hint to the unconscious journey of what our task will be).

When we leave and walk back down the trail, (You may ask- what was the point of all that? The unconscious understands, we are making friends with it.) Don suggested that John (the unconscious minds know the first mind by it's given name, in the 3rd person) place his hands in the snowdrift. Another suggestion acknowledged temporary discomfort from the cold, which will go away. We leave our hands in the snow as ..."we begin to notice that our hands are losing feeling, becoming numb, and we allow that to continue until we don't feel them." (Facial muscles will tell you when this is complete. The muscles will visibly relax and skin color will change).

" I am going to touch one of John's fingers". (doing so). "I would like to speak to the part of John who is in charge of studying". (touching another finger) "I would also like to speak with the part of John who understands authority". "... and the part of John who is in charge of sleeping. And the part of John who understands ambition.. I would like you all, (specified fingers) and other parts of John who are interested, to meet and to discuss and to find agreement. And when you have achieved agreement, I would like that you signal by moving this finger." (Touching another unused finger).

Don went on jabbering about something or other with the class, but keeping the signal finger in the corner of his eye. (get it?-puns are fun in hypnosis, if not elsewhere)

After a few minutes, the finger twitched. Don immediately touched it and said "thank you." Noticing that the finger merely twitched, instead of a strong motion, he asked if they felt confident in their decision. He got a stronger motion. Then he did a count-out.

The next day "John", the med student, reported that last night he had successfully completed his studying plans. When asked, he said he felt confident that he would continue his success. He appeared to be in a more cheerful mood, and his skin color was better. We metaphorically did a productive committee meeting together.

I'd like you to notice that we did not need to find any intellectual answers about what was wrong, or how it was fixed. Nor did we ask that question. It all happened in the unconscious without words, at a deeper emotional level. Remember this evidence of the power of the unconscious minds, when they are in accord. Magic? Not at all.

Part 2- The Model

In addition to the hierarchical Freudian model of id, ego, and superego, let's see if this one augments your insight.

Picture a wagon wheel, with a hub, spokes, and an iron or rubber rim. I don't know how many spokes there are, but I suspect there are as many as we need to have. If not, we can make more.

Is your wagon wheel sturdy and substantial, like a heavy freight wagon; or light and thin, like a carriage wheel? Or quick and responsive, like a bicycle wheel? Make it like you want it.

The hub corresponds to your first, conscious, verbal thinking mind. The executive. The spokes represent all of your unconscious silent minds, each with its own abilities, knowledge, insights, and responsibilities to you. Like department heads. It's good if we can speak with them, and get on the same page. The rim represents the degree to which they are all cooperatively bound together.

I am reminded of Gomez's famous experiments in Learning Theory. He put hungry rats into the hub of a maze shaped like a wagon wheel. At the end of one spoke was some food. The problem for the rat is to find the food.

Now- Classical Behavior Modification Theory predicts that the rat; after finding food in one spoke, will be more likely to return to that spoke next time; having been reinforced in that spoke. But rats are pretty smart about food. Having eaten the food in that spoke, the rat was more likely to search in another spoke the next time. Gomez demonstrated that traditional behavioral theories don't have all the answers. Rats are in fact capable of some abstract reasoning. "The food is gone there, so I'd better look somewhere else."

Each of our minds (spokes) knows what's best about something. Other minds; with other responsibilities, are free to disagree, but if open communicatiobetween them is hampered, cooperation among them in support of the overall good is compromised. They begin to fight, or sulk. We get "symptoms". These minds may try to express their frustrations and wishes in dreams, but we often don't get the message.

Here are some of the special areas of expertise that reside in these other "minds. Sometimes I like to picture these areas of expertise as books on a library shelf. An example of a hypnotic suggestion: ..."Here is the book titled 'Courage'. As you ponder this book, (pause) you come to realize that you know what is in this book. You have done courage before. (pause) You will probably do courage again. (pause) And you can do courage right now if you want to".

Other abilities, that other spokes may be good at, include:

Patient

Loving

41

Assertive

Stubborn

Aggressive

Cooperative

Vicious

Leader (good leaders are agile in all of these,

as seems fittin')

Resilience

Endurance

Strength

Nice

Tough

Passive Resistance

Intelligent (yes, you can!)

Dumb

Attentive

Angry

Dominant? (Careful! Bad things can happen

here)

"Trustworthy, Loyal, Helpful, Friendly,

courteous, kind, Obedient, Cheerful, Thrifty, Brave, Clean, and

Reverent". (The Boy Scout Oath).

And on and on...

You have it within yourself to be good at all of these things, and more. They just require your guided attention, and a little practice. Sometimes we get into a trance and overdo, any one of them. We call that being in a rut. Then we need to get out of that trance, and return to flexibility, like a gymnast. As said before, whichever you do, others will tend to do also. Which do they need, in order to get them back on track?

Most of the time, the unconscious decision about which of these resources to use, is made like a knee jerk, in a microsecond. If you are able to pause for 3 beats, then you will be able to make a more goal-directed decision about which of your resources with which you wish to guide.

Part 3- Implications

Let me tell you a story about ducks.

My friends and I sometimes used to go ice fishing. There was a large wildlife preserve across the river from where we had our weekend cabins. The best thing about ice fishing is that it feels so good when you stop. Stopping for a beer and some delicious heat on the way home puts everyone in a good mood.

The lake on the preserve had a spring on one end that kept a large area of water open, most winters. If the water stays open, there will be ducks and geese that decide to stay, rather than go south. One thing that waterfowl do is eat gravel. Since they don't have teeth, the gravel grinds the grains they eat, in the gizzard. Unfortunately, they sometimes also ingested lead shotgun pellets, which gives them lead poisoning. (this was before lead shot with waterfowl was illegal). They got very sick, and usually died. We sometimes got a sack of them, and took them to a farmer who cared for them in his barn. It was fun to release the survivors in the Spring. It's technically illegal to possess live game birds, but the warden looked the other way. When predators eat lead poisoned birds, the lead goes right on up the food chain.

One day we saw some coyotes on the shore up by the open water. This is unusual in the daytime, so we were interested. And kept watching. One or two at a time, some clearly sick birds would struggle up onto the ice, and hobble to the shore, right into the mouths of the coyotes! What the heck?

Because I was a Psychologist, I thought about this quite a bit, trying to come up with a plausible explanation. I had a few ideas, but after sleeping on them, they didn't hold water. Here's the conclusion I finally came to.

Waterfowl congregate in very large numbers, on water that often becomes contaminated. The spread of disease can threaten the whole flock. It makes good evolutionary sense that they would develop an instinct to remove themselves from the flock when they were sick.

I am convinced that people have that instinct, also. And I suspect that it's a basis for suicidal and other self-destructive impulses. Earlier, I mentioned that "most" of our minds are on our side. This is the exception. When people get sick, either physically or emotionally, you often see suicidal thoughts. If the self-destructive "mind" gains control, it is very dangerous. We need to re-emphasize that warm acceptance and caring, signaling love, can be a life saver to someone in a suicide trance, who feels unworthy of existence.

More on that later, I'm working up to something else now.

Another related story, this one about people who live in tribal cultures.

Mankind has spent the vast bulk of its history in small bands. We evolved our emotional repertoire in small bands of perhaps 20 to 40 people. Larger bands were not viable, because the hunter-gatherer economy could not support them. Also for that reason, these bands were extremely territorial. To allow intruders was simply not an option, to the point of warfare. All pack and herd animals are the same way. Along with this scenario comes intense loyalty and affection, and social order and cooperation, which are some of the things that make us human. Another is that humans developed strict gender-based division of labor and skills, in order to support the inter-dependency and cohesion of the band. They needed each other. They needed no police. (I don't think we should throw our customs away until we know what they were for in the first place).

We are still emotionally adapted to small bands. Large bands spread our loyalty, understanding, patience, affection, and commitment too thin. Patience is like money, if you spend too much of it you might run out of it!. We still tend to react to outsiders and large groups with irritation. Crowds repel us. Especially during rush hour, when we get road rage. I have worked in mental health on several Native American reservations. (They really don't mind the term "Indian", unless they're in a bad mood. They think it's humorous). I, like many other Whites, have felt envy and longing for the stability and serenity of tribal culture. Indians return to the poverty of the Rez, often because they find Anglo culture to be rude, hostile, and crude. They tend to ignore whites on the reservation until they get to know you. You have never been well and truly ignored until you have been ignored by an Indian.

We have become a lonely, annoyed people, and that can make us sick. We each get sick in our own personal way, and that is all you need to know about the myth of diagnosing. I threw my diagnosis book away as soon as I broke free of

46

insurance companies. It's just a prop.

Freud was the first to observe that it is unconscious, unacceptable impulses and resulting internal conflicts that make us "neurotic. He emphasized naughty sexual impulses. Back in the day, people were taught to be ashamed of sex. Women pretended they didn't like sex. (which often turned into a self-fulfilling prophesy). Only ill-mannered men spoke of sex. Now sex is no big whoop, and people are less nervous about it.

Now we are struggling with our native animosity. It is expressions of anger, and hostile feelings, that are socially unacceptable now. And the more the population grows, the more intense, and the more unacceptable, anger becomes. We have this term- "politically correct".

We do have some acceptable outlets for our accumulating animosities. Sports and fitness activities are good. Arts, music, entertainment can be uplifting. Wars offer some relief.

Political parties provide opportunity for shared, acceptable, revulsion and contempt.   Traditional psycho-therapies do provide emotional support. There is a wide variety of stress management techniques that are valid and effective. Assertiveness Training, usually done in classes, can be very helpful. The downside is that you need to keep doing it. More on that topic in a later chapter. There is an old term- "sublimation". It means that the energy of repressed emotions can be channeled into constructive endeavors. Myself, I have a different hobby about every year, usually involving working with my hands. But I think the best lasting answer lies in re-integrating and resolving our feuding "minds".

Our angry emotions originally had a very adaptive purpose. They inspired us to respond to physical threats to us, whether animal, human, or natural. Hans Selye called it the "General Activation Syndrome". Strong emotions such as fear and anger stimulate us, and cause our body to prepare itself for action. Adrenaline and sugar fill the blood. Blood is shunted away from non-vital functions into muscles. Our alimentary systems can vacate themselves. We sweat and flush. Breathing and heart rate increase. Selye is quoted as saying the body prepares for the 3 "Fs"- fighting, fleeing, or feeding. I heard him speak one time, and he actually referred to 4 F's. Fighting, fleeing, feeding, and undertaking reproductive activities.

If the body is too often in this state, or if it is not worked off, it can cause a variety of physical "psychosomatic" diseases of the heart, vascular, and digestive systems. Also warts and rashes.

There is another source of feuding minds that I should mention. It's called "script theory." I should credit Sivan Tomkins with being the first to write about it, although it had

been discussed in therapy circles for awhile. Let me work up
to it.

I had a girl friend once. We were both in the mental health
field, although in different professions. We used to meet
regularly with other mental health types in our building, for
"group," which was our own support and decompression therapy
on Friday night.

Her favorite movie was "Gone With the Wind." In fact, she
was a southern belle from a wealthy family. Our relationship was
sometimes stormy, sometimes I wondered if she was playing a
role in that movie, and I was a support player. Vivian Leigh and
Clark Gable. Take a guess about how our relationship ended.

It is well known that people choose role models, and try to
built social skills and emotional resources and characteristics,
based on those role models. Hopefully, we have many admirable
role models.

We play many roles in our daily lives. We may play one role
at work, another with our spouse, another with our children, one
with our parents, and maybe an entirely different one with our
friends. Are you the same at church as you are at happy hour? It's
like we turn several different people on and off, in accord with
the situation.

And we do it effortlessly, without requiring thought or

intention. This is just one of our unconscious skills. But sometimes we chose entire movies, plays, fairy tales, books, or mythology as models. The danger in that is we can get into a trance with it, and overdo it to the point that it becomes a guiding story in our lives. We can live it to its conclusion, unconsciously, without realizing it, for better or; more likely, for worse.

Working on scripts in counseling (I wouldn't call it therapy) can be fun, even amusing for flexible clients. But it can be a serious flaw in a person's habitual ways of dealing with the real world. We can live out a script, rather than making goal-directed, rational decisions. As a matter of fact I think most people do this occasionally. It is true that in high school, people who are trying to discover their best set of emotional resources, do experiment. They may see an actor, a comedian, a hero, a villain, a leader, an achiever of any kind; and try that out at school to see how other people react to it. Maybe it works for them, maybe it doesn't, but it's a very healthy way to help build oneself, so that we become more effective with other people! We often put labels on our classmates in yearbooks, based on one of their successful roles. (I did John Wayne rather poorly. On the other hand, one girl called me a "high-class hood", and I liked that.). But once again, overdoing it can hamper our flexibility and the development of our own personal styles. Out-of-control (unconscious) trances or scripts usually have negative results.

There is one kind of trance; or script, that can be particularly insidious and destructive, if uncontrolled and taken to extremes. It is called Passive-Aggressive. At the extreme it is called Anti-Social Character Disorder. It can result in individuals, or even whole families, becoming isolated.

What it consists of is the habit, or trance, of passively interfering with other people, in such a subtle way as to avoid being caught at it. These people are habitual obstacles. It is nevertheless an enactment of aggressive impulses. It is a form of revenge. (Did you think I wouldn't get back to the point?)

Think of words like obstructionist, contrary, negative, slow, playing dumb, disagreeable, stubborn, resistant; often with a sweet smile of innocence. Maybe a smirk of defiant challenge. They become masters of being obstructive and in your way, and are often ironically judgmental of others. Picture the overly-cautious driver who's answer to every circumstance is to stop in the intersection, or the person at the salad bar that must have just one more piece of lettuce, and the only one that will do must be at the bottom of the bowl. Or the one who makes a defiant entrance into the party, exuberantly late.

They rob us of our time, which is the only thing we have that is truly ours! You are being punished for existing, and for trying to do your own things without permission. They are joyous when you express consternation, because that proves to them that it is you, who is being difficult.

We all know how to do this script, if the situation warrants! (C'mon- admit it. Can you honestly say that you have never done it)? It is when it becomes a lifestyle; that is when it becomes pathological. To the extent that people don't realize that they do it, to that extent they cannot get out of that trance by themselves.

Insurance companies won't pay to treat it, because it's considered untreatable. It is just so deeply buried, and these clients are just so naturally resistant anyway, that clients disappear when you get close to it. What can you do about that?- merely avoid it if you can.

If you are a therapist assigned to treat it- diagnose something else, like everyone else does. (I'm only half kidding)

Ask your client- "What are you doing?" Then follow along with them-. Some of them might lead you to themselves, and to the trance which controls them. We can deal with trances that are out of control!

In this thing we call "reality therapy" (Glasser), we ask- "What did you do about that problem"? (wait for an answer) "Did it work?" (wait for an answer). Then let's us try something else? (implication being that we need to come up with a better idea.)

If I've blown your own cover about the above Passive-Aggressive trick, then good for you. That means that you are aware, and that you are in control of your own self.

If not, then I hope you have plenty of Prozac (registered trademark) or something. Such as that can help you to remain blissfully befuddled about what is happening to you..

As my grand pappy said: if mom ain't happy,- ain't nobody happy".

It is that our aggressive and our angry impulses which are our own, which challenge us to our own time. (Notice the hypno-language there).

Usually, our cognitive and intellectual insights don't work very well with all of that.

The rest of the book will focus on what <u>does</u> work. In the next chapter, we'll explore a general purpose relaxation exercise and trance induction script.

For those of you who are interested in further the-oretical debate about hypnosis, go to: http://en.wikipedia.org/wiki/Hypnosis#The state versus non-state debate

Chapter III

An Example of a Hypnosis Script

What follows is a script. I usually don't use scripts, because I prefer to remain free to go into trance with my clients, and respond to their present needs, as I read them.

Often, clients will tell you where they would like to go. Conversational, script-free hypnosis was pioneered by Erickson, because it has no fences around it. There is something more elegant about it.

But I almost always use this one for openers, especially when I'm working in front of a group. People generally like it a lot. It has the advantage of making it clear to participants just what a trance is, and what it is not.

It also shows people how easy it is to trance. They learn how to do that (Or maybe I should say that they remember how to do that. Have you ever observed children watching Sesame Street)? and subsequent trances are faster and almost effortless, like taking a deep breath.

If you still feel some trepidation about hypnosis, try this. Record this script in your own voice (merely speak slowly and calmly), then find a calm, quiet place, and play it back for yourself. What have you got to lose? Doing that might also give you confidence to do it for others.

Here goes.

(This exercise will produce a deep state of physical and mental relaxation in about 85% of the people who participate. The re-learning of the ability to relax will remain indefinitely in most participants.)

In this written script, I will underline the most important words. These words carry a power to stimulate mental imagery which supplements the relaxation response, and they are repeated often. Also, explanatory observations (such as this) will be marked off with parentheses, so that the reader can have a sense of what is happening. Words to be spoken aloud to participants are marked with quotation marks. Feel free to use your own words, it is not necessary to memorize these exact words. Call them merely suggestions.

"This is an exercise intended to <u>help</u> you practice the relaxation response. You don't need to do anything except to be here. I will ask you to use your <u>imagination</u> to form <u>pictures,</u> or to think about words in your own mind. This will allow you to re-discover the part of your mind that knows how to <u>relax.</u> If you decide not to participate, you can certainly do that. You might <u>simply</u> find it <u>interesting</u> to observe what the rest of us are doing."

"What we will do is set a mood which allows you to <u>explore</u> the <u>parts of yourself</u> which <u>listen</u> to your body. The ability to <u>relax deeply</u> brings with it some healthy benefits. If you choose to go along with the mood we <u>create,</u> you will feel much like you do when you are <u>deeply engrossed</u> in a television show, a movie, or a good book. You will be fully conscious and <u>very aware </u>of what's going on around you, but you will probably be unconcerned about noises or interruptions. You can continue to <u>relax</u> if you wish."

"If you wish to participate, I would suggest that you close your eyes. That makes it <u>easy</u> to experience what we're doing. I know that your eyes are not accustomed to being closed for long in the daytime, or in company.

In a moment, - - I'm going to ask you to <u>allow</u> eyes to close, but you may notice that your eyes may want to flutter a bit until they become comfortable. Eyes work very hard nearly all day long, and they may not be sure that being closed is OK. You can simply think about "relax" as you focus your attention on your eyelids, and in that way you will know that your eyelids are comfortable when they no longer feel like fluttering. That means that they agree to relax and be comfortable for a while". (Here we are using repetition , both to reinforce what we are saying, and to stimulate a little bit of boredom, which puts one's mind in the mood to wander. Pause 5 beats)

"But for now, let's think about breathing. Can you remember when you last took a nice deep breath? Let's take a nice deep breath and as we <u>let</u> it out, also allow your eyes to close along with it. (Demonstrate with your hands that you are taking a deep breath, and letting your eyes close as you release it. Up and down motion, slowly.). "Now take another, and open your eyes as you do, and <u>allow</u> them to remain closed as you ...let it go. That's good, they can feel the <u>ease and comfort</u> of being <u>allowed</u> to close. Now take another breath, this time breathing deeply into your chest, and also continuing to breathe deeply into your abdomen, for a fully complete breath."

(From this point on, it's good to gradually begin to speak

more slowly and more softly. You want your voice to become gentle but clear, so that it is not disturbing at all. Also, begin to allow your own breathing to be heard in your voice. Begin to allow natural pauses in your speech to allow for breathing. Make it easy, without strain. I like to pace my own breathing with someone in the front row, which helps keep it natural. The listeners will come to match their own breathing pace with yours, and that will help reduce the feeling of separateness, or otherness, between us.)

"Notice how your body likes to breath and relax. (pause). "And as you continue to relax, focus your attention on the muscles behind your eyes- - the ones that work hard all day in moving your eyes and watching things. (pause). Simply allow these muscles behind your eyes to relax- gently and easily- requiring no effort (pause.) "You might bring a picture of- loose - rubber - bands to your mind's own eye. (pause.)"And this picture will be a signal to those muscles, meaning that you allow them to relax (pause). "Requires no effort. Let them enjoy being quiet.

(Your listeners are now in a light trance. In a trance, a person's eyes often role up into their head. If that goes on for too long, it may result in muscle strain and a slight headache. This suggestion, of loose rubber bands, prevents that.)

"And as your eyes continue to relax, focus your attention on the muscles in your jaw. Notice that there is tension in those muscles. Jaw muscles like to chew. "Simply allow those muscles to feel relaxed - - warm and heavy. Requires no effort. Simply allow those muscles to enjoy being allowed to relax for a bit."

"And as they continue to relax. Allow the muscles in the back of your neck to relax. Warm and heavy - - requires no effort (pause). Let them keep just enough energy to keep your head up. Relieve them of all unnecessary tension. Lightly balance your head."

(From this point on, you can put in as many pauses as you feel will give people time to contemplate. Your voice will know the good times to pause, and you can let your voice decide. You are also in a trance now, and the participants will be listening to you somewhat uncritically, because they have begun to trust you. They will be relaxed and passive. The only thing you can do wrong from here on, is to use a word or suggestion that is unacceptable or annoying to the participant, in which case they will immediately stop doing this, snap out of the relaxed state, and look at you as if you betrayed them.

When I learned to do this, we were in the ballroom of a large hotel. A waiter came in and began to noisily fill water glasses. The instructor simply said... "and you can simply ignore things that do not require your attention". And of course we did).

"And allow your shoulders to relax. Simply allow them to relax deeply. Warm and heavy, requires no effort. You can allow your shoulders to relax very deeply. Shoulders can be relieved of the weight. Let your shoulders fall toward your chest.

(Repeat the above, but put in "upper arms", then "lower arms", then "hands". Pay some attention to fingers, which are first to become tension arthritic Feel free to vary the wording, if you get tired of listening to yourself. When you get done with that the participant will be bored by the repetition. Their conscious mind will be hungry for something interesting to think about, or to happen. Their mind may begin to wander, and they will be in a dreamlike mood. Their unconscious mind will consider and accept suggestions which it agrees are good ones – (and no others).

"Now allow your fingers to relax. Notice how joyous that fingers feel the welcome relief. (this may sound silly, but it makes perfect sense to the fingers mind). "Warm and heavy. And isn't that interesting!"

"And allow your upper chest to relax and calm. You notice that as you allow your upper chest to relax and calm, your breathing wants to have some of your attention. And that's OK, give it whatever attention it requires. You can continue to calm very deeply, in your body - and in your mind".

"And you can carefully pay close attention to my voice, or you can carefully ignore my voice, or neither, or both. The important thing is simply to experience what you are experiencing".

(As the conscious mind tries to escape this baffling wording, it allows a deepened trance, and also focuses attention inward, upon the self.)

"And you are able to continue to relax and calm your lower chest. It is particularly healthy to bring your stomach into the calming, because we don't often listen to the stomach unless it is uncomfortable". (This is a general suggestion for people who tend to eat too fast, and therefore to overeat; because the stomach's satisfaction response takes some time to kick in. The unusual phrasing strengthens the suggestion).

"And allow your lower back to relax and join the calm. Notice that your lower back requires some energy in order to remain erect. That's OK, allow it to use whatever energy it requires, as you continue to calm even more deeply, in your body, and in your mind."

(Here, we have suggested; twice, that the mind can join the body in the fun and in the learning. Participants are now starting to realize that they can do this by themselves, without you. Good! They may begin to pay only superficial attention to what you are saying, and hear only the name of the body part that is joining in. They are probably exploring their own minds, and may be doing lucid dreams, or daydreams. In this mood, they are open to constructive suggestions. One of the things that interferes with human communication, is that people can be so busy in planning what they want to say next, that they can't actually listen. In this mood, they have freed themselves to listen. We can try to do a little humor, because we are having fun).

"Allow your upper legs ("limbs", in Britain) to relax and calm. Warm and heavy, requires no effort. And your knees. Notice that your knees, because they work hard, are able to enter into the knowing of the joy of our calmness - - and that the learning of that is both new and old. And isn't that interesting. Things can be re-realized".

"And allow your lower legs to relax, and your feet. Toes, in particular, like to relax. Notice the looser and easier flow of warming blood to your toes. (With tension, blood flow is restricted in legs. Causes cold feet).

"Your feet will thank you if you allow them to enter into this more often, and they will feel gratitude to you for showing them this way." ("gratitude" means that I am more likely to get paid! Bodda- bim, bodda-boom)! But seriously, folks-, I have actually said that at closing banquets at workshops. Laughter doesn't hurt anything. Participants might be a little awed by this, but it brings in the OK-ness of playfulness. Laughter is both a cause of, and a response to, reduced anxiety and tension. This suggestion makes the participant an active partner in adopting the relaxation response as a long-term skill. The "cold feet" metaphor will be recognized by the unconscious, and is a strong anti-anxiety suggestion. Also good for diabetes and forming romantic relationships).

"And as you continue to enjoy the deepness of your relaxation, in your body and in your mind, imagine a powerful relaxing force, which enters through your toes, flowing in, much like warm water. Allowing your feet to feel the soothing of it more deeply. Wiggle your toes." (Here we are demonstrating to the participants that they can flow into the agility and the into dexterity to go into, and out of a trance, at will. They are in easy self-control. Wiggling toes is also fun).

"And the powerful relaxing force continues to flow, filling your feet and lower legs, flowing much like warm water, warm and heavy. Continuing to flow into your knees and upper legs, allowing them to relax and calm more deeply. The relaxing force flows into your abdomen and chest with the quiet power of calmness and confidence".

"The powerful relaxing force will flow up the back of your neck, relaxing as it goes, and flow across the top of your head, and it comes to rest , to abide, in your forehead. - - Your eyes can remember that".

"And as you continue to enjoy this experience, there may be a place in your body which is still tense. Let your mind look through your body until it discovers the place that is still a little tense. Let it roam".

(I , me own self, tend to carry my tension in my shoulders. Everyone is different. If you watch, you can see the stiffness in peoples' parts as they walk.)

(Pause until you see some response).

"Now you can focus the calm, relaxing force to the place, and you can allow it to gently relax the place."

"The powerful, calm, and confident force will always be there, and you can use it whenever you like. It can even come to help, when you are not even thinking about it. It belongs to you, and it is yours".

(Count out).

(Now we need to show that something actually happened. If we ask if people if they feel like they "have been hypnotized? "Raise your hand." About half will not raise their hand. That's because a trance is so usual and ordinary to us that it doesn't seem unusual. We do it all the time.

Ask those who raised their hands to describe what they felt.

Here are some tricks of the trade- . As the audience gathers, you will notice that at least one person will show the grey skin color, furrowed brow, and dark eyes of a tension headache. After our trance, ask them "what happened to your headache?" You will hear, "It's gone!", with facial expressions of amazement).

"That's good. I wonder how long that you felt like it took?"

(People will guess that it all took about 5-10 or so minutes.)

"By my watch, it took 40 minutes."

(This is because; during hypnosis, our internal clock is suspended. Athletes who use hypnosis training report that it appears to them that their opponents are moving in slow motion.

Once, after an hypnosis workshop, I was speaking with the instructor, and I mentioned that I was not looking forward to the 8-hour drive home. So he talked me down into a light trance, and gave me the suggestion that I could do this while driving, so that my clock could be suspended. I did come out of the trance in order not to forget to make 3 turns. You can do that. At one point in the mountains, a fox jumped out in front of me, and I was on the brake before I even realized it., and I was amazed at how fast my reaction had been! Research demonstrates that reaction times are faster with trance. If I had waited until my conscious mind made a decision, the fox would have been history. Anyway, as I pulled into my driveway, it seemed that I had been driving for about 20 minutes)!

In this altered state of awareness, The brain naturally produces an array of chemicals, called neurotransmitters. Some of them have a chemical structure that is similar to opiates. Yes, they are "feel good" chemicals, and they improve our mood. It has been shown that the group of natural chemicals in the brain called endorphins, reduce or even block pain. Strangely enough, when persons are encouraged through guided imagery to concentrate upon moistening their mouth by increasing saliva (the "lemon" image works well), the they report less pain. Nobody knows why that works that way! It has also been shown that when people feel pain, different parts of the brain are active than when they are ignoring pain. We can stimulate those "ignoring" parts of the brain with hypnosis. Knowing that, we can then view chronic pain as merely an opinion! Or a decision, made at a deep level. We can learn the skill of changing that decision or opinion.

Some of the antidepressant medications; in fact, work by altering the amount or function of these chemicals in the brain.

There is a big downside to artificial neurotransmitter medications. The brain learns to compensate for them over time. In the case of serotonin re-uptake inhibitors; for example, the brain gets lazy and begins to produce less serotonin naturally. Then, when the medication is discontinued, it takes the brain some time to get back "in shape." That means a time of unpleasant symptoms. That's one of the reasons that these medications are not recommended for long term use. One of the maxims of Biology is "Use it or lose it". It's dangerous to fool Mother Nature.

I think that anyone who is thinking about using psycho-active medications should consult the "Physician's Desk Reference" at the library, and learn the downsides to them.

I have done the above trance induction so many times that I can stimulate these chemicals in my brain at will, almost instantaneously. I can't tell you how I do it, that would be like trying to teach you how to balance a bicycle, without having a bicycle to practice with.. The only way to learn it is to do it. The best way is to visit a hypnotherapist, most of them have some variation of such a progressive relaxation in their repertoire. You; yourself, can also record the script in your own voice, and play it back to yourself. Just find a quiet place to lie down, where you won't be interrupted. All you need to do is follow your own instructions. It's easy. As you do this, you may notice some awkward phrasing or other things that seem uncomfortable to you. Feel free to change them, as you wish. Make it yours. Above all else, make it yours.

The above script can be varied as you like. You can slip in useful suggestions to suit your audience or your client. Once a client become accustomed to trancing, you can use shorter inductions, such as counting down on an escalator, deeper and deeper. If you want a client to speak with you , you can ask them to come back up a few steps to where they can be comfortable in speaking. You can also go to different imaginary places and times, when you get to the bottom of the escalator. We can do that. Many people can do it if you just ask them to, and give them a few seconds.

I will present some other trancing scripts later in the book.

Chapter IV

Hypnosis and Medicine

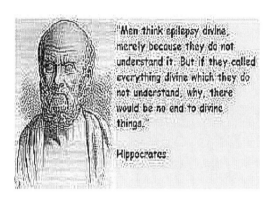

"Men think epilepsy divine, merely because they do not understand it. But if they called everything divine which they do not understand, why, there would be no end to divine things."

Hippocrates

In the introduction to this book, I mentioned Milton Erickson, M.D. Dr. Erickson had Polio as a child, and was paraplegic and confined to a motorized wheelchair all his life. In order to combat the pain, he taught himself how to do hypnosis. The result was that he pioneered and perfected a new method of hypnosis, one that does not rely on gimmicks, gadgets, or other hoopla. He simply entered into ordinary conversation with his patients. (we say "patients" for people under medical care, and "clients" for other therapists. When I get referrals from physicians, they are his patients, and also my clients).

Milton would gently lead them into the world of fantasy, imagination, and possibilities. In the universe of our minds, all things are possible.

Milton had a slight speech impediment. He never would answer the question whether it was the result of his Polio, but many of his students felt it was a plus in hypnosis, causing people to focus on his voice and on understanding him. It certainly wasn't necessary, though.

Dr. Erickson liked to start his classes with a few brief assumptions that he brings to therapy:

1. The patient is making the best decisions and choices available, given the options available. I once asked if this applies to severely psychotic patients. He responded that severely psychotic patients really have no options available, at least until their medications are stabilized. He looked at me as if to say "naturally!", and I guess it was a silly question. Focus your emphasis on the word "options". That idea is central to Ericksonian therapy. He had a gift for leading people to discover more options in their lives, and that gift is learnable.

2. If a needed option or solution existed at the patient's conscious level of awareness, it would have already been implemented. This fact implies that we will need to get to the patient's unconscious minds.
We must do something to engage with unconscious processes.

3. The patient has many skills, insights, and behavioral

resources in the spheres of their experiences, that can be brought to bear in the present. Memories of these presently dormant resources can be recalled during hypnotic trance.

4. Nominalization. In the English language, it is more difficult to describe and discuss emotions, than it is in some other languages. We need to give each relevant emotion a name, as a form of shorthand. "Angry" might be turned into irritation, annoyance, madness, disappointment, hate, etc. This name might even be a made up word, known only to the two of us. One client used "the pricklies".

5. Presuppositions are used instead of commands, as hypnotic suggestions. "As your other minds search for new, or old, ideas; you can pay close attention to my words, or you can carefully ignore them. The important thing is to experience what you are experiencing".

6. Confusion can be used to stimulate imagination. This can take the form of ridiculous associations, preposterous stories, obvious illogic, puns, metaphors, double meanings. People tend to mentally escape this discomfort by daydreaming, and that's a trance.

One of my favorites- "...and it doesn't make sense to think about humor when you have the pricklies". (In a later chapter, I will discuss this in more detail, with examples.)

7. Negative commands. Negative words tend to be ignored and dropped by the unconscious. Words like can't, won't, isn't. There is a negative suggestion in the last sentence of #6 above. The word "doesn't" will be ignored.

8. Mind reading. This was Erickson's term. Most hypnotherapists call it "pacing", or "active listening". It is very intense focusing on the patient, involving not only their words, but body language, motion, expressions, breathing, even changes in skin color..) It is really just heightened perception and awareness. (I will expand on active listening in chapter IX).

There are many stories about Dr. Erickson that are told by his many students. He and his students founded the Erickson Foundation in Phoenix, and now we have fourth generation students teaching around the world, some on tour. Many have written very good books, and you can get them at libraries or online. Just search "Milton Erickson".

Just a couple of my favorite stories:

After Milton retired and stopped accepting patients, he looked out the window and saw a lady sitting on the edge of his fountain, in the garden. The previous day, she had knocked on his door, literally begging for his help. Milton's secretary; of course, told her that he was retired and sent her away. So here she was at the fountain, just waiting, and had been there all morning. She was just staring blankly and waiting. Milton could see that she was off into the wild blue yonder, and was in a trance.

He decided to go out and see her. His buzzing wheelchair rolled up to her, and she opened her mouth to begin making her plea. He waved her off, saying "Just go back to where you were before I came". And she did.

(Do you have a picture of Milton's fountain in your mind? Water is so basic to life, that the mere sound of it; real or imagined, has a calming effect on our minds.)

Another. There was a young boy in the hospital for safe-keeping. He had been acting up: running away, stealing, etc. Milton read his records, and could understand that he was locked into a spiritual siege with his parents. He was fighting to establish his own identity and his self-direction, in the only way he knew. He didn't have the words to explain himself, so he resisted his Psychiatrist. He was a very miserable lad, as were his parents: "How do we get through to this kid"? As it was, Milton was conducting a workshop at the hospital auditorium, and he arranged a demonstration for the class with this boy.

Picture the auditorium, full of people in white coats, with clipboards and stethoscopes.

The boy is sitting on a three-legged stool in the middle of the stage, with lights on him. The psychiatrist is briefing the audience on the case, explaining that Dr. Erickson, the famous do-things-to-people guy, is going to come out and do something (In the boys mind, something mysterious and probably unpleasant) to the subject. This poor kid is now dumbfounded, and wide open to suggestions.

So Milton buzzes out, stops by the stool, and looks at the boy for a few beats. Then he says "I don't know how..."

Here he pauses. (The boy is completely blanked out, since the mighty guru says he doesn't know how)? ..." you're going to improve your life." Then he turns and buzzes off.

Afterwards, it was reported that things got a whole lot better in that family. The boy had indeed come up with a better strategy, as suggested. I would imagine that it came to him in a dream. We don't really need to know what it was. But the boy will always know that he has it within himself to solve his problems.

And isn't that interesting!

But most physicians don't like to talk about hypnosis. There are several rational reasons for that. Let me explain.

First, it doesn't make economic sense for them to do hypnosis themselves, even if they were trained to do it. Some physicians have been known to see 20+ patients per hour. That's 20 office visit fees, compared to just one for a hypnosis session.

Physicians do not like to work by the hour. Even psychiatrists try to avoid it. The typical psychiatric office now has a number of "ancillary" therapists to do the hourly work. This leaves the psychiatrist free to do more lucrative fee-for-service work, such as hospital contacts, electroshock treatments, consultations, and medication checks.

Physicians also do not like to obviously fail in front of their patients. With hypnosis, there is always the chance of blatant failure. They are, after all, the MDeity. (I don't think I'm being unfair here. My own students have called me "PHDeity".

Today, in the United States, most physicians work for large corporations, governed by business managers. Neighborhood family physicians are becoming rare. House calls, which were once a concrete demonstration of the dedication of physicians, and were also a confirmation of the intimacy of physicians over the generations, are extinct.

Make no mistake, Medicine has become a profit-oriented big business, like any other. The hospital-based corporations, Medicare, the few large health insurers, and the A.M.A., all cooperate to impose a near monopoly upon the business. They share this very big pie among themselves, by means of contractual agreements. There are rumors of kickbacks, and even criminal prosecutions.

Even if a physician; there, wanted to do hypnosis, the red tape involved would preclude it. Making an outside referral for hypnosis services would amount to heresy. Physicians in corporations do not send money out to people who don't work there!

The other sad thing is that hypnosis helps to improve treatment. One example is in the treatment of cancer. It is now recognized that hypnosis provides real, measurable improvements in the course of cancer, and increases survival,, and even remission. If you find that hard to believe, do a web search on "cancer and hypnosis", or "Oncology and Guided imagery". There are a number of scholarly books on this topic, in addition to the clinical research. There are some private hospitals that emphasize it.

In fact, it is well recognized in Medicine and in Psychology that all; yes- all, diseases have a stress component. The reduction of stress tends to enhance and to stimulate healing. Stress is also a statistical predictor of the incidence of disease. Many surgeons refuse to do surgery until the signs of stress in their patients are back to normal levels.

Calming is; of course, central to hypnosis. Remember that I am retired, and that I don't have a reason to lie to you.

Let me tell you a story about myself, in order to build up

to a point. Bear with me.

I had received a rifle wound in a hunting accident, and my hip bone was fractured. The surgeon said the bone looked like a fractured windshield. The stupid thing I did after I got out of the hospital was go fishing. Now, the water in the hull of a fishing boat is not clean, so sure enough I got an infection, both staph and strep. Before it was all over I had been in the hospital for six weeks, and had surgery four times. While there, I was not expected to live, in fact they called my parents to come from 600 miles away.

The surgeon spent some time with me every day. He said I could have as much pain medication as necessary, and I could keep a bottle of scotch in the refrigerator if I wanted. At the time I was the director of a mental health center, and we knew each other by mutual referrals. I told him that I didn't want any chemicals, because I did self-hypnosis, and chemicals would interfere with that. I also did guided imagery to stimulate and guide my immune system. Many of you may not remember one of the first video games, called Pac Man. In it, there are little yellow faces with big mouths, that chase little creatures around a maze and gobble them up, one by one. In trance, I pictured this process repeatedly, with the suggestion to my white blood cells and immune system to do just that to the infection bacteria. A side benefit was that the six weeks went by in what seemed like just a few days.

I didn't take anything for the six weeks, and (obviously) I survived. He was amazed by this, and we spent a lot of time talking about hypnosis. He told me that he had often wondered if; at some level, patients under anesthesia were unconsciously aware of surgery.

"They must be", I said. "The brain and nervous system must stay awake enough to keep the vital life processes going. Otherwise breathing, heartbeat, etc. would stop and they would die! The unconscious parts of our minds that do those things are very aware of the state of our bodies, especially when something happens to it."

We went on the next day talking about the frequent bizarre behavior, after surgery, of surgery patients. They very often are confused, paranoid, grouchy, even abusive to staff. They don't sleep well, and eat little. They often avoid social contact, even friends and relatives; and seem to wander around aimlessly, some-times even leaving the ward. They need to be watched.

You can imagine how traumatic it must be for the parts of our mind that take care of our body, to realize that: "Holy cow! Somebody is cutting me up and dismantling me, and I can't wake up"!

Actually, the unconscious thinks of us in the third person, by our given names. So when we talk to it, we don't say "you", we say "Martha", for example, when referring to the conscious part of Martha. So the quote above should read... "I can't wake Martha up!"

The good news is that it is pretty easy to prepare the unconscious for this experience before surgery. It only requires a light trance, because the unconscious is very aware that Martha is very nervous, and something serious and mysterious, probably something bad, is going to happen. It is very interested in finding out what!

So we make an appointment for "pre-surgery guided imagery". We also want the surgeon to be there, if possible, because the patient has already made a commitment to trust him/her, and will likely do whatever the surgeon suggests.

We begin with a short, simple relaxation trance induction. If the patient is comfortable with eyes closed, that's probably enough.

"And now I would like to speak with the part of Martha that is concerned with her body. Martha, you may listen in if you like, but the important thing is that you simply allow the part that cares for your body to hear."

"There is a problem in your body. (The unconscious already

knows this very well, but it will be glad to hear that somebody else knows it also. You can describe the problem, if you like.) The surgeon is going to open the body so he can fix the problem. He will first give Martha some medication that will put her to sleep, so that she will not have to feel pain. You will not be able to wake her up until the medication wears off. He will ... (here put in a brief, simple explanation of what the surgeon will do. Use simple words, the unconscious doesn't have very much of a vocabulary.)

"You will be able to carry on with caring for Martha's body. When he is finished , he will close the opening, and you may begin to heal it. You will be able to wake Martha up, shortly after that. Is that OK?")

(Here you are likely to see a very slight nod of the head. If you see the eyelids flutter, it means that the unconscious is still not sure, or perhaps is confused. In that case, do a deeper relaxation, maybe go down the escalator to a calm, relaxed place. You needn't be nervous; you can't do any harm here. Consider doing the "glove anesthesia" described earlier, asking for a signal when you have been understood.)

"One other thing. You will want to bleed, so that you can cleanse the opening. That's good. But if you want to help the surgeon, you can slow the bleeding, because it might get in his way. He will cleanse the opening". (don't mention that the surgeon can see better with less blood, because this part of the mind can only see what is in Martha's mind, and doesn't really understand the word "see" like you and I do. Another caution-you probably haven't noticed that there are no negative words in most of the scripts in this book. That's because the unconscious simply ignores words like "not, can't, don't, no, won't", etc. It's like it erases them. For example- don't think about pink elephants!) Surgeons are amazed that the anti- bleeding suggestion usually works!)

Like Erickson, Mike Hunter was also a physician, hypnotherapist, and author. He would demonstrate how easily and reliably that a person with a hypnotically anesthetized hand (glove anesthesia) could control blood flow. He would insert a large sterilized needle through the skin of the back of a subjects hand. (don't do this unless you are a physician). He then would ask the subject to predict which side the hole would bleed from, thumb side or little finger side, after he removed the needle. He even asked some to predict whether it would bleed at all. I never heard of an instance where the prediction failed to happen.

For reasons cited above, your surgeon is not likely to mention hypnosis or guided imagery. You need to ask. Medical folks like to grant your requests, unless there is a reason to not.

Let me digress for a while, and talk about the mind /body connection.

I once taught at a University with a very large Psychology Department. We had some undergraduate classes that drew as many as 1100 students, who attended classrooms all over the campus, connected by closed circuit interactive TV. They were also divided into small discussion groups, each with an advanced graduate student.

We also had optional, elective laboratory classes in Psychology. We worked with white rats, to demonstrate a variety of principles of learning. Each student had her/his own rat, to work with and care for throughout the semester. Prior to the semester, I would prepare the rats by allowing them to feed freely for a few weeks, and then I would weigh them to determine the "free-feeding" weight. Then I would reduce their food so that they had stable weight of 80% of the free-feeding weight. This is a healthy weight, but it did make sure that the rats were actively interested in food.

In one of the demonstration experiments, we used what is called "T" mazes. These are long boxes with paths for the rats to run through, and T intersections, so that there is a correct and an incorrect way for the rat to turn, right or left. Each maze had a clear plastic lid, so we could watch. Each student and rat had a T maze. There is only one path to the exit, where some food is waiting for the rat.

The maze was also wired, so that when the rat made a correct turn, it was automatically rewarded with a pellet of food. Conversely, if the rat made an incorrect turn, it was punished with a slightly uncomfortable electric jolt to its feet.

We divided the class up into 2 groups; those who's mazes were rigged to provide only punishment for incorrect turns, and those that were rigged to provide only reward for correct turns. The mazes kept records about such things as number of errors, number of correct turns, and number of trials until learning. (learning the maze was defined as 3 consecutive trials without an error). This is not a fully controlled experiment, because we didn't have enough control groups for comparison, but it was close enough for demonstration purposes. Here's the result.

The rats which were rewarded learned the maze consistently faster, with fewer errors, and fewer trials, than the rats which were punished. It was the same every semester. Not only that, but some of the punished rats developed behavioral problems. They did not like the maze, and sometimes they would bite the students when approaching the maze. The students had to wear thick gloves.

The punished rats also got into more fights in their cages in

Genetic Biology is: How do cells develop individual structure and function? As soon as an egg cell is fertilized, it begins the process of dividing into more cells. Each cell contains precisely the same DNA

inheritance code, half from each parent. Each time there is a division, twice as many cells are produced. This process of growth continues to the point when the cells begin to take on specialized functions. Some become skin cells, some liver cells, some nerve cells, some bone cells, and on and on. How do they come to know what they are to become, since they are all genetically programmed exactly the same? How is this decision made?

No one knows for sure. We can only speculate. There must be some form of communication that acts to provide such instructions, which is not differentially contained in DNA instructions! The DNA instructions are all exactly alike in all the cells! It seems that these cells are somehow communicating with each other, and are "discussing" the matter! This points to some form of rudimentary awareness or consciousness, and decision making.

If you wish, you can demonstrate this cellular communication to yourself.

Get a bag of jelly beans, the ones with multiple colors and

with multiple flavors that match the colors. Taste each color, and notice it's flavor. Do that a few times. (Don't get carried away, save at least half the bag for our experiment.)

Now close your eyes, reach into the bag and select a jelly bean. Hold it for a moment in your fingers. Rotate it. Now try to guess either it's color or it's flavor. Take it out of the bag and check to see if you were right. If there are 6 colors/flavors in the bag, the laws of probability say that you should be right, about 1 out of 6 times. Now, if you get it right, go ahead and eat it.

If you were wrong, put it back in the bag. If you keep doing this, you will find that the skin on your fingers keeps getting better at recognizing which color/flavor it is holding. If you really like jellybeans, you can work up to 5+ out of 6.

It is a known fact that some cells in the skin are sensitive to light. Somehow, they learn to recognize color quite accurately, and somehow they communicate this information to your brain. (It is also known that some skin cells can recognize pheromones. Pheromones are chemicals that give a distinctive odor to sexual hormones). That may be a part of why sexual dysfunction occurs more often when it's not the right partner.)

Some mathematical calculations indicate that evolution happens too quickly to result only from natural selection. The development of the human brain is a sterling example of evolution that happened in a comparative split second, on the time scale of evolution. There is evidence that some of our hominid ancestors ate the brains of their dead, like our rats above.

As stated above, it is difficult to think of a medical condition that has not been shown to respond to hypnotherapy/stress reduction. There is a great deal of research on the topic that has accumulated. A web search on the topic will bring you more research reports than you probably care to read. Your public library has professional search engines that can focus on very specific research topics, and they like to help you with them.

But here are some of the symptoms/problems that respond most dramatically to hypnosis:

Anxiety

Phobias

Habits and substance abuse

Hypertension

Intestinal symptoms (ulcer, colitis, spasms)

Pain (especially head and spine aches)

Tension, chronic fatigue

Anger, hostility, resentment, irritability

Stroke/paralysis

Hyperactivity/ learning problems

Stage fright

Insomnia

Overeating

Obsessions/compulsions

"In general, I believe that no condition is out of bounds for trying hypnotherapy on."

Andrew Weil, M.D., Arizona Center for Integrative Medicine.

"Despite substantial variation in techniques among the numerous reports, patients treated with hypnosis experienced substantial benefits for many different medical conditions."

James H. Stewart, M.D., Mayo Clinic College of Medicine.

Chapter V

Sports and Performance Hypnosis

Lars Eric Unestahl, Ph.D., was an instructor of mine in
hypnosis, and was also the hypnotist for the Swedish Olympic
Team. He was also faculty in the Department of Psychology at
the University of Orebro, in Sweden.

As a researcher, he has compiled statistics about the
performance of his hypnosis-trained athletes over the years,
compared to athletes who did not train with hypnosis. (Lars called
it "Inner Mental Training)" You readers who are trained in
scientific method might recognize a research design flaw here. It
can be argued that the athletes who volunteered for hypnosis training might be more motivated than those who did not, and therefore
their performance cannot be causally attributed to hypnosis alone.
On the other hand, lack of motivation is certainly not characteristic
of Olympic athletes. Researchers know that there is no such thing
as a perfect research design.

Lars' student athletes built up some impressive statistics. For example, 29% of his students made the Olympic team. Of that 20%, 58% were finalists. Of those, 67% were medalists. There are many more stats that also demonstrate impressive improvements in various performance scoring methods. He also conducted structured, intensive interviews with many athletes who had demonstrated instances of unusually outstanding performance (even for them). The great majority reported some kind of "altered state of awareness." Opponents appeared to move in slow motion; the goal looked to be twice its regular size; legs felt dramatically stronger; it was easier to get through the pain and endurance wall; it wasn't necessary to consciously remember training, because it was just automatically there, as examples.

While it is true that some amateur coaches hire hypnotists, and most professional coaches do, it is true that in the United States, hypnosis is not as well recognized or utilized as it is around the world, in older cultures. Below are examples of hypnotic training used in other countries, along with what it is called there, and a noted researcher/author.

Brazil Terpsicho Trance Akstein
        Therapy

Another advantage of doing this is that it provides us with the words and images that the client uses to organize h/his thoughts and memories. When we speak with h/him in hypnosis, it will be helpful to speak in the personal style of expression of the client. The client has; in fact, already provided the outline for a hypnotic script.

If the client has not yet had the experience of an example of outstanding performance, we can build together a fantasy experience. ... "Imagine what it would feel like to...".

(After light trance induction, by any of the techniques in this book). -

"I would like you to remember the part of you that recalls this experience, and I would like you to imagine it again. Let's go to where your body and your mind can go there and do that again, as we ride down an escalator to where you can be deeply relaxed. Counting down the escalator from 10--9--8--7--6 (At some point here you will get some signal from the client that the trance is deep enough. Any motion or change of facial expression is a signal).... and we can stop at the place where you can remember easily, requiring no effort, and to speak if you wish to." (From this point, we have a moderately deep trance; remember to use the given name of the client, i.e. "John" when referring to the first mind, instead of "you".)

"Let's go back to the huddle. It is late in the game, and it is 3rd and long. You can sense the concern in the eyes, and in the bodies, of the team. You also sense determination, and that lets you know that they are prepared for max effort. You have also seen some hesitation in the strong side linebacker, when a short receiver is in jogging motion to that side. The coach knows this."

"The call goes to John (you; we are speaking to the other mind, now), on that side, as you and John hoped it would. You begin to prepare for the play, in your body, and in your mind. You rehearse it in your mind, as you take your position. The crowd hushes as the count begins."

"The ball is snapped, and the handoff is smooth. As you run down the line, a gasp and a cheer is heard from the crowd. Out of the corner of John's eye, you note that the defensive tackle is off balance, but in the wrong direction. You immediately alert john to this, as you sent to your legs the strength, agility, and quickness that will be needed to snap into the different hole. Strength, agility, and quickness. Your legs are burning with strength, agility, and quickness, like a compressed spring that wants to be unleashed, and you feel the unlimited power in them. (mixed metaphors are OK, and even a fun tension reliever). The defensive line looks to you as if it is moving in slow motion."

"John cuts toward the hole with the strength, agility, and quickness that you have sent to his legs. John leaps through the hole with the power, into the secondary. You (unconscious) are aware of the roar from the crowd, but John is too busy to notice it. You can remind him later."

"As John had anticipated, the linebacker took a step toward the outside, to cover the man in motion. He is now a step out of position, without momentum. Taking advantage of this, John is just too quick for him to recover. John is now running free, and you both feel the joy and the power of it."

"The safety now commits to trying to angle John. He might catch John, he might not. But he cannot match the power of your determination and your resolve, unless you allow him to. You have given your mind and your body to the power, and John has given you back the ability that you wanted, so that you both have prevailed as a team. You feel the confidence of that, -and you are as calm about it as last year's bird nest. Just hold on to the ball."

(Just a little fun here, to prepare for the count out.)

"I am going to suggest to John that he can call upon you, and the power, when it is needed. I am going to suggest that he use the word "calm" to signal you to what is needed. Just the word "calm". (In fact, I have already suggested it.)

"And as I count from one to five, you will be able to comfortably return to the here and now. As I count, notice not only how relaxed and refreshed you feel (2-- 3), but also notice that the power belongs to you. You have used it before, and it will be there for you to use again. 4,-- and, --5. Take a moment to get your bearings."

The above general outline can be adapted to any sport. Now that you know how it works, you can also use your creativity to adapt it to the particular, specific needs of an individual athlete, with consultation with that athlete's coach. When I used to race stock drag cars, we looked for the one strategic point of intervention, the next one component where the most gain can be found. As an example, most athletes (and most everyone else) tend to carry their tension in a particular part of their body. You can see which part it is if you closely watch them walk and move. Picture President Nixon, giving the "peace" signal. Can you see the tension in his shoulders? It can be any part of the body. Over time, that tension can turn into rheumatoid arthritis. It tends to be symbolic- e.g. -in people who feel ineffectual or angry, it often goes to the fingers or arms.

This native tension, which tends to get tighter during competition, is counter-productive. Muscles work in pairs, and tension in one requires equal and opposite tension from its pair. This is a waste of power and energy - the body is working against itself. Plus, it makes us awkward and off-balance. We need to focus the "powerful relaxing force", discussed earlier, on that place. For a lot of athletes, this should probably be the first strategic point of intervention.

Golf requires a great deal of muscle coordination. that is more important than strength. A great many strong, muscular golfers envy Tiger Woods' drive. He makes it look almost effortless. When you watched him drive, you could see that his muscles are in perfect accord and focused on the results. The muscles were clearly not arguing with each other, and the result looks almost poetic. Only when he was under a lot of stress, and probably tense, did that kind of power wane. The same is true of gymnastics. Baseball has more of a cerebral element, requiring a talent/skill of anticipation. We can do anticipation.

A catcher; for instance, needs to be able to visualize where every player is, in any situation, even if his back is turned.

Often, shortstops seem to anticipate where the ball is going, even before it is hit. Some batters will tell you that, when at their best, they can tell which kind of pitch is coming, just by being hyper-tuned into the pitcher's subtle movements, balance, and body language. Distance bicycle racers/ runners simply cannot win without the ability to trance, and they would not last for long in those sports without it. Otherwise, the pain is not endurable. Sometime, you might watch swimmers, or skiers, "meditate" before events. Divers may spent achingly long periods of time at the back end of the board, until they feel that they have their muscles, and minds, reliably on board. They are working with their minds. Athletes sometimes call it "the zone". I have the opinion that with intense military training, such as SEALs, "making the cut" would be improved with hypnosis training, beforehand. I think it would work at least as well as yelling at and shaming the losers, like boxing trainers and drill instructors do.

But, we could go on and on with this.

Let's do another script that is good for abilities/ performance in general, and can be adapted to fit the athletes needs for performance, in any field.

We need to do a light trance, in whatever way the client is accustomed to. We will deepen it as we go.

"We are sitting under an apple tree on a hill. The sun is shining between slowly drifting, fluffy clouds. A Meadowlark is singing, as we relax more deeply, in our body and in our mind. The Lakota Indians are fond of relating that the cadences in their language is similar to that of the Meadowlark."

(We've done this before, but every time I do it, it comes out a little different. Go with your mood. Your clients will like it better that way, too. I never make chili the same way twice, neither. Do as much sensual visualizing as seems right at the time. This script is better slowly, with lots of pauses).

"We notice a carpet lying on the grass nearby. We can tell it's a magic carpet because of its oriental design, and the magic lamp resting upon it". (We are not going to do any wish-granting genies here, we are just stimulating the story-loving visual fantasies of the child within. The "magic" will come from within, not from genies, and not from me."

"Let's rest upon it, too. As the carpet begins to rise, you notice that the lovely country scenery begins to unfold. You can see the pattern of light and shade , as the white clouds drift across the sun. The birds easily do not notice you, because you are only a daydream.

You can relax deeply, because you are perfectly safe here."

"In the distance you see a gleaming white marble building, glistening in the sun. Isn't that interesting. By your will alone, you can guide the carpet toward the building, because you are curious. The carpet gently comes to rest on the ground below a short staircase."

"Curious. You walk up the stairs, wondering what the white building could be holding. As you enter the large bronze doors, you notice all the books, arranged neatly on the shelves. It must be a library! What a lovely, quiet, cool (say "warm" if it's Winter) place, with velvet drapes and wood paneling and leather seats."

"In a corner is a door with a staircase leading down. There is light there. (get it)? The unconscious is very good at metaphors). There are seven steps, count them as you step down, in your body and in your mind."

7...6...You are able to regain the powerful relaxing and calming force as you step. 5...4...3. And calm as deeply as you wish. 2... And...1."

"You see a single cozy corridor, with a bookcase to the side. It is like a private place. Because it is private, John (remember, it's good to use the third person name, because that's the way the unconscious experiences your client If you don't feel comfortable with doing that, it's not necessary to do it), can look at the titles in order to discover what is here in this private place. One is titled "Calm", and John realizes that he knows what is in this book. He has done Calm before, he will probably do Calm again sometime, and he is doing Calm right now. Another is titled "Inner Knowledge". John knows some of what is in this book. He has discovered things about himself; his skills and abilities; his strengths and weaknesses., and he will probably go on with that learning in the future. Another book is titled "Courage". John has done Courage before, he will probably do Courage again, and he can do it now if he wishes."

"As you (talking directly to the unconscious now) look over the titles of the other books, recall a time when you felt that you were at your best. Take your time, because we want a time and place when you didn't fully realize that you had access to these books, about you. There is some combination of these books that; together, describe you when you are at your best.

"For example, there are books about assertive, or intelligent, or humorous, or attentive, or agile and quick, or about articulate, and so on." (Chose these to fit your individual client; whatever they came in for in the first place)."Take some time to select a few books that you like." (If you watch closely, there will be a subtle change of expression, or a slight muscle movement somewhere, when the client is ready to go on.)

"That's good!" Now select them, and walk over and place these books on the shelf next to the earth globe in the corner. (pause). "

"But you notice that it has no continents on it. It is just slowly shifting areas of color, that are lit from behind. It is attractive, and you feel like touching it. As you do so, the colors become more vivid, they move around faster, and the light increases."

104

"This is your source of power and energy, and it contains as much power and energy as you want. You can feel the power and energy flowing into your hands, into your body, and into your mind. It also flows into your books, giving you more control over your body, your mind, and your books; giving them the power and the energy, to be at your best. Take as much power and energy as you want. "And you realize that the globe belongs to you. You know where it is, and you can use it whenever you want to. You can even take it with you if you like, because it is yours."

(Count out, we're finished with this session. We don't need to come back on the carpet).

In your own office, you will want to make a good impression on others, especially the boss. Your achievements are important, but most of the people there are not aware of your achievements, not fully. They probably don't pay much attention to your memos. It is in face to face meetings that people form most of their observations about your capabilities and your value. Your style of communicating in meetings then becomes of central importance.

"So you will want to be at your best there. And you can focus your power there. Begin by recalling your last meeting. You might be able to recall that you wished you had spoken, but for some reason you did not speak. You had good insights and ideas, but something kept you silent. Perhaps you did not wish to interrupt someone who had taken the floor. Perhaps you were not sure of your words. But you later regretted not speaking. It was a lost opportunity."

"And consider that lost opportunity for a moment, and keep the picture of it."

"Myself, I recall watching a meeting with President Kennedy and his Cabinet. Before ending discussion on an issue, he called upon each Cabinet member, and asked if they had any additional words. He didn't want unspoken knowledge to be overlooked. He did that before deciding about what to do about the Cuban missile crisis. But- most meetings are not like that. Most are free-for-alls, with many good words left unsaid."

"Now recall a meeting where you made a good point and scored some points. There may have been a brief moment of silence in the room, as people realized that you had perceptively moved the debate forward a notch. Something was settled, and the room was free to move on. It was progress with the issue."

"Perhaps you took command with words like-

"I have had experience with that" - or

"That lies within my field" -or

"I would like to speak to that."

"You did this with the power and the energy that

you recall is there within you. You radiated that power and energy from your body and from your mind. Your eyes showed the confidence that was in you, and all of them there could see it there."

"Now take that picture and reduce it into the bottom right corner of your mental screen, so that the picture of the Lost Opportunity, again fills the rest of your mental screen. Do you have it there?"

"Now when I say "ZAP", I want you to reduce the Lost Opportunity picture to the bottom left corner of your mental screen, while at the same time you can fill your screen with the power and energy picture."

"Are you ready? OK- ZAP."

"And now you may keep that picture, so that you may have it whenever your confidence can use it, and the power and the energy will come with it."

(count out). Another technique to consider is to guide you client through an actual meeting, coming up in the future. We can rehearse points to be made, and strategies with which to make them. A light trance enhances calm dialogue, so that we can visualize and imagine, back and forth between us.

Sales is another area where we can make use of ourselves and our powers within. If you know your clients well, you can form some opinions about where their sales skills might fall flat. You can even ask them to describe their strengths and weaknesses, which they can probably do with a light trance! They have probably thought a lot about that. You can make use of these insights to tailor you hypnotic script for them.

In sales, it at some point becomes necessary to take the lead of the conversation. This usually comes a few minutes before the close. Without that command and control, the customer is free to reflect on his/her doubts and hesitations, and the result of that is "Let me think about it". That almost surely turns into a "No".

All of the suggestions in the above script about meetings are also relevant to sales. What's the difference, really?

"As you continue to contemplate your past successes and failures, perhaps you could tell me about some of you sales meetings that did not go well?"

(Listen closely to the stories. Feel free to ask leading questions, because a light trance is really only a mood; an atmosphere. There will be good clues to help you compose your suggestions. Take your time, it's important. Then go ahead and do the same with the successful stories.)

Again, your client has provided you with the outline of a script. Walk them back through the patterns that emerge in the stories, in order to emphasize differences in how the client handled them. Bring in the intense radiation of strength and power from the body and from the mind. Reinforce the pictures, as above. "Calm", and "relaxed", are also good suggestions for sales. You might use what I call the "babble" technique, which I will talk about in the next chapter.

The response that you can get from the following question; might strike you as "magic"!

At the end, before the count out, ask your client:

"And how do you go about forgetting the difference?"

Then sit back, relax, and let the client tell you all about that.

You are likely to hear that intense anxiety can throw them off their game plan, for example, so then you can work with that.

Chapter VI

Fun with Puns, Duble Meanings, and

Cunfusion

In the FAQs section I mentioned that the strange, even silly language of hypnosis is not for every client. It is distracting and even annoying to some. It can; however, be very effective with those who enjoy it and find humor in it. Example- "I know that you believe that you understand what you think I said, but I wonder if you realized that what you heard is not that which I meant."

I also mentioned that a trance is nothing more than the state of mind, or mood that we enter whenever our first mind is engaged somewhere other than the here and now. Let me expand on that for a moment.

The first mind can also be otherwise engaged by playing with language in unusual ways. The client can become involved with words and meanings, and become confused and entertained. Even though that **is** paying attention to the here and now, it is also engaging the first mind in "something else", and therefore leaves the unconscious minds free to come out and play. These minds are the ones who are looking for fresh ideas. (suggestions). They can contemplate and evaluate suggestions, in the quiet time, when the first mind is doing something else, or is being quiet.

Another downside to this technique is that it requires prior planning and memorizing of a script, and that doesn't allow the hypnotherapist to go with spontaneous instincts that are based on his/h knowledge of the client, and her/h reading of the current state of the client. (that's called "pacing"). Some hypnotherapists don't agree with what I just said., and that's OK.

Let me offer some of these "confusion" scripts, as examples. Perhaps the best known practitioner of this approach was Kay Thompson, D.D.S., and I found these scripts (or ones like them) in my notes from one of her classes. I would also like to thank Rosalie Williams at Crown House Publishing for confirming that these do not appear in Dr. Thompson's collected works. I have done some editing with them.

Music

"There are a lot of things going on inside your head (say "heart" with Native Americans), at any given time...but for a little while you can deliberately put them aside, and just absorb, like a

111

sponge. We talk about a lot of different ideas, that fit into some of these learning experiences that you have had, in ways that you and I may not even understand right now. But that's all right, because we don't really need to understand.." (Here we are implicitly asking the first mind to bow out of the conversation).

"And as you wonder about them, it's nice to think about things with a curiosity, and to wonder about what's out there, waiting to be tested and explored, discovered, felt, appreciated, reacted to, and as you let yourself do that, you find that you also become a little more aware, of the differences between your body and your mind, between your attitudes and your feelings, between your conclusions and your other possibilities."

(Here we reinforce the willingness to re-consider our biases and pre-conceived conclusions. Some say that insanity is doing the same things, over and over, and expecting a different result).

"And that when you sit there, you find out that you can be very much aware of your body without being aware of your body at all! And you can almost float with your mind, up and out of your body, to a corner of the room, and look back and observe your physical self, that it is You that is presented to other people. And that's why we have to learn about the You that is presented."

(We are talking about, and paving the way for, the benefits

of self-contemplation and self-awareness. My grand pappy
said... "Time spent in solitude is never wasted.")

"My job is to reflect on your job, and to offer some options
about it, that your mind can work with, think about, and listen to,
to learn. It's almost as though you were listening with your mind
to some music that is very, very interesting... the way you listen...
because you can listen to that stereo in stereo, and if you focus on
one instrument, one theme, you can feel your body flowing with
that sound, that music, that feeling, that color, that mood of that
one instrument. Or maybe it is that group of instruments, all the
same."

(You can use actual music if you like, but Dr. Thompson
chose not to. I think that was because she was very confident).

"And then your attention recognizes that while you thought
you had been listening to that one, other instruments had been
playing which you hadn't paid attention to as you listened, but
suddenly it becomes relevant to relate to the realization of the
other sounds of the other instruments."

(The idea of alternatives, again. Are you feeling sleepy,
yet?)

"And you can tell when there's a discord because you can
hear what needs to be done when you listen. Or you can back off
and listen to the music as a whole, and you can let yourself sink

into that hole, to be submerged in the loveliness of the
experience. The sensitive sounds, the creative color, the emotion
of feeling that wells up in the surrounding."

"And we can hear and adjust the tone and tune of any discord,
slowly and methodically adjusting and refining our performance.
We accept the clear, true harmony of working together, of playing
together, with the delicacy of the result depending upon all the
balance within. Then the majesty of the instruments and their
harmony, their ability to create an uplifting aura for the ears,
comes into play. And the color, the swell, the work in hearing the
beauty of the result are worth all the work that goes into its
creation."

(Is "swell" an outdated adjective?)

"And each part is the instrument that is necessary for every
other part to be at its best, and so very soon we find, in us, that
that instrument is an instrument that contains the potential for
helping all the other of the orchestra to produce the right kind of
sound, without each individual organ playing in harmony there
would be nothing but discord."

"An occasional discord offers a learning kind of situation,
because the organ that is not in discord can turn to the one that is
not in tune but in discord and say, "Hey, shape up, get in time,
get in tune, so we can sound good together."

(Is she suggesting confrontation and conflict? Read on for the alternative. Also, we have a somatic metaphor here).

"And gradually the discordant behavior is modified and changed, and sometimes it takes a long time, because the discordant notes keep trying to jump into the good, true sounds. And they should not do that, because they mar the whole. And so the true sounds, and the true notes, are able to maintain their own integrity, their own sensitivity, their own individuality. And by virtue of being the way they are, by being their own sounds-good, sweet, clear, true- gradually they can shape their sounds around the other discordant sound, permitting it to be modified just by listening, just by hearing, the kinds of things it can learn to do, and to hear, and to be."

(Confrontation is another form of discord).

"And as you let yourself float along, submerged in and surrounded by, the glorious , harmonious sound, recognizing the worth of your own contribution, just by being yourself. And for the people for whom you sound right, they can accept your offer to let the sound surround them, for their own learning."

"It is very nice to be able to know that you have the capacity to make the appropriate kind of music, whatever it might be. And when you're making that music, it's interesting to think about it. Sometimes you may take a guitar string, on a guitar, and you know that guitars can require a lot of warming up. And if one of those strings is a little loose, it just can't make music at all when you plunk it. There is nothing. But one of the other strings, where there is too much pressure or tension, trying to play it is only a painful shriek. Somewhere in the middle ids the right tension, and it makes the sound just right. And somewhere inside of you, you know that you are able to walk around without any tension, so that you make no sound at all.

And you also know that you can walk around with so much tension that it shrieks."

"It seems true that the world keeps trying to make us more tense, when it shrieks at us. Maybe sometimes we need that, maybe sometimes we don't. And so, inside yourself, where you can listen, you can hear the right tone. You have learned the tone that is right for all the tone, the amount of tension, the muscle tuning, and you know the tone that goes with all the right things happening in your body and in your mind."

(Count out).

So, how did you react to that? Personally, it seems to me to be a little on the ambitions side. It contains many suggestions, some subtle, and some not so subtle, but it seems to contain so many suggestions that many may not sink in. Like a sermon.

116

I used to play the bass drum in a bagpipe band, so I appreciate
the impact of a single, clear, tuned boom at precisely the right
time. Maybe I'm biased.

This one suits my own style more.

Wine Making

"If you think about it when you drink wine, no matter what
kind of wine it is: do you take wine as a matter of course, or do
you ever think about all the effort that goes into making wine?
It truly is an amazing procedure."

"First of all, the vines must be for the proper grapes, and
must be planted in the proper place, so that they have soil that is
neither too sour nor too sweet. Then we hope that the vines will
get the right amount of rain, and the grapes get just the right degree of sunshine, with the good cool nights coming at the end of
the growing season."

(As my grappa used to say: "All things in moderation,
including temperance".)

"Then comes the time, after nature has done her work of
growing the grapes, for man to step in and start the process that
will produce the wine. It is traditional to have a special person,
who knows exactly when the grapes are at their perfect stage of
readiness, ripeness, and sweetness, and knows they are perfect to

be picked. That someone checks the grapes, and teaches the grape pickers how to select each bunch, and sometimes even each grape. As the pickers choose the grapes, they carefully pick each bunch by hand, and then they place them carefully into the basket."

"After the grapes, in their pick- of -the- crop condition, are taken inside, it is time to bruise them, and break their skins. Only in this way can they start the growth and the fermentation process, which happens when the natural yeast, that is always there on the grapes, is given the opportunity to come into contact with the sweet fruit."

"Now is the time to decide whether to make red wine, or white wine. For red wine, the grapes are allowed to ferment with the colored skins, for white wine the colorful skins are removed."

"After that first fermentation process is completed, the next step is to press the grapes, because you need to separate the juices from the solid materials. The fermentation process continues, but any air must be kept out of the process and away from the juice, because, during this fermentation time will spoil the juice, and you will get vinegar."

"When this bubbling and working fermentation process slows down, then we know that it is time to filter the wine to remove sediment. This is done more than once, because the fermentation is continuing. Then move the wine to a new container, for a new start. As wine ages, with this help, it purifies and clarifies. It goes on as long as it is really working, and at just the right time, the fermentation of the sugar may be stopped by very fine filtering, which removes the yeast. Do we want sweet wine, or do we want dry wine?"

(At this point you are probably quite bored, and have begun some unauthorized daydreaming)

"And it's really exciting to wonder what that wine can become, because the juice bubbles with creativity and the opportunity to grow and change, and we know that in a year or two, or however long it takes, there will be a fine product, well worth waiting for. Only then is it put into individual bottles. And the fascinating thing about this is that the product, each year, from the same variety of grapes, can be so very different. It is all dependent on the grapes, the soil, the moisture, the sun, and the picking and processing. And it is all so very good."

"So, when you have your next glass of wine, take the time to think about it, to smell and distinguish the aroma and to really appreciate that aroma; to roll the wine around on your tongue and inside your mouth, so that you can enjoy the explosion of that

controlled, contained quality and determine its distinctive characteristics. And when it finally is swallowed and absorbed, to
permit that warmth to permeate your senses, so that you know
that it is worth all of the growing pains, all the bruising, all the
pressure, all of the fermenting, all of the trouble of the process,
because the final product is so perfectly enjoyable. And the glow
of the aftertaste continues, not only in your body, but even longer
in your mind, and in the ways that you go about planning
yourself."(Oor- you could just put some grape juice in a glass
jug, put a balloon over its mouth, and wait for the balloon to
deflate.)

Chapter VII
Identity and the Dumb Blond Syndrome

Everyone needs to be somebody.

It was Shakespeare's Falstaff character who concluded that if he could not be the world's greatest lover, he would become the world's greatest bastard. He was unabashedly vain, gluttonous, intemperate, boastful, thieving, and cowardly. But we love him anyway. In "Henry IV" Prince Hal comments about him:

"Wherein is he good, but to taste sack and drink it?

Wherein neat and cleanly, but to carve a capon and eat it?

Wherein cunning, but in craft?

Wherein crafty, but in villainy?

Wherein villainous, but in all things?

Wherein worthy, but in nothing?"

But we love him anyway.

People spend a great deal of time and effort in developing

their personalities; the roles that they become good at playing. We try out different roles, and carefully observe how others react to them. In the teen years, that becomes nearly a full-time effort. Think of any descriptive adjective that can be applied to people's behavior, and I'd guess that you have tried it out at sometime.

Other people have a strong influence on us as we go about this personality-building. Their expressions of approval and disapproval provide us with feedback in our search for self. It is called the "self-fulfilling prophecy", or the "Pygmalion effect", when we become what others expect of us. (the film "My Fair Lady" was based on the play "Pygmalion". We try to train each other to be socially acceptable, amusing, or; at least, in compliance with our favorite biases.

The downside of this process is that it also can reinforce self-destructive or negative behavior. A child who is told that h/she is lazy, stupid, careless, ill-mannered, etc., is more likely to develop such traits, especially if they discover that negative attention from others, is better than no attention at all. Or- that it can be amusing to others. As mentioned, everyone needs to be somebody. We have a strong tendency to live down to our reputations. Most drill instructors know better than to call a recruit weak or cowardly.

Stereotyping other people often has this effect. In our popular legends, we can all think of the popular stereotypes of the people from each and every nation. Pause and think of the stereotype of your own nationality? And; there is a tendency for them to start acting that way. We like our blonds to play dumb, and they often do. If you expect your employees to be shirkers, some will sense that, and obey your perception of them. Allow me to suggest that you re-read this paragraph. I'll wait.

I mentioned earlier that we learn to play different roles for all the different people in our lives. We behave differently at work, at home, with friends, at church, with parents, with employers; for just some examples. This is an unconscious process of automatic adaptation, unless we stop to think about it. And as such, it is really a trance.

And we can- stop to think about it. It's just that sometimes we need a little help in order to do that.

There have been several hypnosis authors who have observed that; quite often, the problem is not helping someone get into a trance, the problem is getting them out of a trance that does not serve them well. There are good habits, but there are also not-so-good habits. Habitual non-productive behaviors are also trances. We need to become aware of them, before we can get the heck out of them. The difficulty; of course, is that people have a very strong tendency to reject advice. We all play "yeah but, yeah but" at times. My dog is very good at it. Sometimes we even respond to advice with rancor.

So; as hypnotherapists, we need to come up with a better strategy of persuasion. Remember the "glove anesthesia" script from an earlier chapter, with fingers representing our different "minds"? (we could also call them our different automatic trances). That's one appropriate approach to getting out of a negative trance. It's really just a way to get people to explore unconscious alternatives in their habitual behaviors, without annoying them or criticizing them. There are other approaches to working with habit trances, which we'll get to a little later.

Let me go back, and build up to the next point.

Have you ever discussed a disagreement with someone, and after you gave your argument, had them say anything like "I see your point. I never looked at it like that. I guess you're right"?

Doesn't happen, right? I once said that to a friend, and he looked at me for a moment, and said "You condescending *#@&%!

It seems to me that there are very few people who are willing and able to change their minds, at least not openly. It's as if we view changing one's mind as wishy-washy, or weak, or an admission that we were wrong about something in the first place. Nevertheless, just about everyone is willing to admit that they had been wrong about something in the past! (but not now). We revile politicians who change their mind, even though most people will agree that the willingness to change one's mind is one of the most mature things that a person can do! (but not me). In the land of academia, scientists are willing to tell you that they love to discover that they were wrong, because that is scientific progress. Yet if you look closely, you will see that most of them will fight bitterly against changing their mind, and will negate any idea or information that was not theirs, or is not the party line. Actually, I can't think of any other group of people that is so hostile toward new information! (except for that other political party). Learning; itself, is a process of finding the things that we are wrong about, and changing minds. But yet nobody thinks that getting an education is a sign of weakness! You cannot learn anything with your mouth open. Many people take classes in Active Listening. Active Listening is simply sending signals, both verbal and non-verbal signals, that you are listening carefully and that you want to hear more. If you do that well, people will tell you about surprisingly personal things. They often say things about themselves that that they didn't realize to begin with.

Sometimes we give to others the time to talk. But there is still our habit of using the time we give others to talk, to just think about what we are going to say next. Another trance.

Why do we get caught up in this kind of doublethink?

Our tendency to reject any implication that we should change our mind, and discount any person who implies that; is precisely why psychotherapists and counselors avoid trying to give advice. That's like trying to teach a pig to whistle. It just wastes your time and annoys the pig. (I didn't intend to dis my clients.)

It simply doesn't work. I think maybe we could all agree that if we became better at seeking information and contemplating evidence that might lead to changing our minds, then that alternative trance might make the world a better place to hang out in.

We are much better at it if we call it "exploring alternatives". Magic words- nothing wrong with that.

I once worked with a family that was having discipline and obedience problems with the oldest boy. Nothing unusual in that, but they were locked into a severe contest of wills. The father was bent upon thinking up new and clever ways to punish him. The son was equally stubborn in thwarting him. Each agreed that the other had a "whim of iron". They came in after a very ugly battle over washing the salt off of the boat after an outing. Mom just listened to them while they threw angry accusations at each other, with a look on her face that said she was trying to keep her patience.

It has been said that insanity is doing the same things over and over, and still expecting different results. Sometimes we expect that people will comply with our wishes if we just get angry enough. (I have never done that, of course). Both father and son had logically plausible positions; it's just that their methods of debate were building very hard feelings.

I had a few sessions with them, both together and separately, but I was not making progress in getting them to think outside their buns.

So I decided to try some Ericksonian hypnosis. I got father and son together in my dark, peaceful office (I had a rheostat so I could turn up the lights a little when I could perceive insight in my clients. It's like a metaphor). Erickson was famous for conversational hypnotherapy, without formal trance induction

I began with a long monolog about anger, peace, obedience, authority, compliance, manliness, etc. Anything that came to mind; the point was to bore them into their own world of escape fantasy. You can see it in people's eyes when they are escaping into their own world. The "thousand yard stare".

When I saw that , I quietly asked the boy to stay in that more comfortable place, and to take his own time in exploring the fantasy of a better dad, out loud, for us. I had given him some

carefully.

On lonely nights apart, each was to light their candle. "You can go ahead and resent each other; and eat and drink, but first you must blow out the candle."

Encouraging the contemplation of alternatives and possibilities can be very simple. I used to keep a box of small brass sticks with a cut glass crystal mounted on one end of them.

I'd give them to clients, calling them "your Miter". This is a pun, and the unconscious is the first to recognize puns. It here's "Might-er". A miter is actually a bishop's hat, but who cares. I'd ask them to bring their miter to each meeting, and when I asked them to take it out and look at it for a moment, that was the signal to go into our contemplative trance, the "what if?" mode, and out of our "yeah-but" mode.

Another way to overcome your tendency to avoid changing your mind is to teach yourself to dream about your problems and questions, at night. It's quite easy. Go to a hypnotherapist and request guided relaxation imagery All of them can do that, each in their own way. Once you learn to deeply relax, you can do that when you go to bed. Then just give yourself the suggestion to dream about whatever it is. Ask for alternatives from your unconscious mind. You're likely to get them. You might not remember them, but they will live on down there anyway, and you will notice that you feel more confident about your problem or question.

Here is a way to check in with your unconscious minds, to see if they are ready and willing to re-consider habits; or even decisions and attitudes. You can do this by yourself, but it works more dramatically if someone helps you. It's easy, and reliable. Let's say that "Nancy" says that she would like to quit smoking. Well and good, but the reasons for smoking in the first place, are likely to go deeper than Nancy's first mind realizes. We may need to discover hidden objections to the idea of quitting, in her

I have an Imperial Topaz crystal (any interesting object will do), which is mounted and suspended from a gold-plated pendant chain, about 12-15 inches long. It can swing freely in any horizontal direction. I introduce it to my client, explaining that there is nothing magic about it, it is merely a way to ask questions of the unconscious. It should be emphasized that there is no paranormal power at work here, such as psychokenesis, or anything like that. That part of Nancy's mind that knows about and controls smoking can easily cause the pendulum to move. That part can influence subtle and unconscious muscle contractions in the arm and hand, in a regular manner, causing patterned motions of the pendulum. Nothing spooky, here. This is also the phenomenon behind Ouija boards. I demonstrate how easily it swings, placing my right elbow on the desk, allowing my right wrist to relax, and dangling the crystal to show that it can swing freely.

"Now you try it."

I move her arm to the same position, pat it reassuringly, and give her the "Pending Pendulum".

"Now I would like you to relax comfortably, and play with the pendulum a little, to see how it swings. It requires no effort."

"Focus your attention on the crystal. Ask yourself-'Are you ready to become a non-smoker". ("quitting" is a threatening word). Out loud, ask Nancy again if she is ready to become a non-smoker. Again?"

"Good! Now repeat the would 'yes', over and over, out loud. Good! Do this slowly until the pendulum begins to move."

(The pendulum will begin to move in some small way. Repeat with the client the word 'yes' until the motion becomes more pronounced, it will start to have a regular motion-perhaps a circle, maybe back and forth, or forward and back, whatever. When the regular motion is clear and obvious, hold her hand and say: 'Very good!- that means 'yes').

"Now let's do the same thing again, but this time let's find out how to say 'no'."

(repeat the process above, substituting 'no').

"Now let's go back and ask Nancy the question. Repeat 'Is Nancy ready to become a non-smoker'? And Again."

Slowly, a clear yes or no answer will appear in the motion of the pendulum. The client will be amazed, and confident that unconscious processes exist, and therefore can cooperate.

If we get a yes, we are ready to go on exploring the process of changing the habit. If we get a no, we can explore the objections. We'll go on with Nancy in the next chapter.

This technique can be used for virtually any question that can be in one of two words; Good-bad, red-green, up-down, etc.

I once had an instructor who demonstrated with a couple the suggestion that they trade dreams after they were asleep at night. The next week they came back to the class, and were much more animated and interactive with each other, even touching each other.

You might ask your unconscious to suggest back at you, something that you might consider changing your mind about.

133
Chapter VIII

Illustrative Cases

Below are more cases which you may enjoy. I have selected
them for illustrative value, in order to provide an overview of the
range of applications for hypnosis. They are actual clinical cases,
but disguised.

A. Elizabeth, Fear of Flying.

This was actually my very first hypnotherapy client. I had
completed several courses in hypnotherapy and was eager, if
also intimidated, by the prospect of actually applying this new
tool in my toolbox.

I was the area director for a largely rural 4 county are region,
and managed offices in 3 local towns, under the supervision of
the administration in the main, central city. Elizabeth lived in a
town about 60 miles away from my home office, and there were
no other behavioral health facilities there. She had to wait for a
week to get an appointment with me. It was my habit to do the

initial intake interview myself, rather than my (young) staff, since intake information is critical to treatment planning.

Elizabeth had no history of mental or emotional disturbance. Her presenting complaint was a phobic fear of flying. When the aircraft engines would start, she would go "white-knuckle" and hyperventilate. She feared losing consciousness. Her last attempt to take a short flight was so excruciatingly painful, that she had given up on ever flying again.

Now her husband was scheduled to deliver a professional paper at a convention in Las Vegas, and she desperately wanted to join him. She was proud of him, and wanted to show him that.

Our time before the convention was limited. It was clear that we could not afford to begin the course of long, traditional psychotherapy. Results would simply be too late in coming. The process of exploring her early memories, events, and probably all the complexity of her relationship with her husband, would just take too long.

I knew that the recovery rate with hypnosis is very high with phobic symptoms, so at the treatment planning meeting two days later, I tried to make the case with my boss and my peers to utilize hypnotherapy. I was worried that he might refuse, and take the case himself. I was, after all, inexperienced. But he was very supportive and readily agreed.

When I saw Elizabeth again, I explained what we had decided to recommend. And of course, she expressed some trepidation about hypnosis; she knew very little about it. So I tried to explain it; what it is and what it isn't, and to answer all of her questions. She seemed satisfied.

So I decided to spend some extra time with her, and we did the progressive relaxation guided imagery which I described in an earlier chapter. This was to introduce her to hypnosis, and pave the way to our next session. At the end, when I counted her out, I noticed that her skin color had changed; from grayish to nice healthy pink. She also had been rubbing her forehead and temples, so I knew she had had a tension headache. That is not at all unusual, when people are entering a strange place with a strange person, and they have no idea what is going to happen.

So after she had yawned and stretched and become re-oriented to the here and now, I asked: "What happened to your headache"?

She dropped her jaw in amazement and said "how did you do that"?

So I could see that we were "off to the races", and that we were going to achieve a good outcome in short order. She asked for another appointment the very next time I was in town. Again, we had little time. So I invited her up to my main office in the next county, and that's where she came to meet.

She knew how to cooperate already, so the trance induction did not take long. Together, we walked into the airport, through check-in, out to the plane, took a seat, and the engines started. This is where her symptoms kicked in. She was extremely uncomfortable.

I went into an Ericksonian monolog and took control in order to give her some relief. I spoke about how I saw her extreme tension as a good thing, since it was a fact that her tension was the only thing that was keeping the engines running, keeping the wings attached, and the plane in the air, If she relaxed for even a moment, the engine would quit, the wings would fly off, and the plane would fall! A slight smirk at the corner of her mouth told me that she recognized the irony of what I was talking about.

I then mentioned that it appeared that she carries her tension in her forehead, her chest, and in her hands. We then escorted these tensions into her back, down her torso, and into the chair where she was sitting; and there we told them to reside.

After count-out, I asked her where her tensions were. She replied "In this chair".

"So why are you still sitting there?" Up and out she went.

A few weeks later she showed up in my office with brownies and iced tea for the staff. She said she had a wonderful time, and actually enjoyed the flight. She had never looked out of an airplane window before. I got a nice kiss on the cheek.

B. Marge, So what now?

Marge was a cattle ranch wife, who lived many miles away from the nearest neighbor, and nearly an hour's drive from the nearest town. She was senior, and her children and grandchildren had moved to the city. They would "ride fence" in an airplane! She was bored to the bone and lonely; She said her most enjoyable time was the Fall branding, when the ranchers and hands would all gather to share the task of branding the calves. They would hire a band, and barbeque whole sides of beef. Big doin's! There was a crossroads bar a few miles away, but she did not consider that to be fun, and disapproved of drunkenness.

She called herself "depressed", but she had showed none of the physiological symptoms of true clinical depression. She said "There's only one important thing left in my life, and I ain't ready for that." I did not refer her to a physician for anti-depressant medication, because I had other plans for her. (Any medication tends to dull a person's response to hypnosis).

After a few sessions of what we call "supportive Therapy" (as if it were an actual entity), and some progressive relaxation guided imagery, to get her accustomed to altered states of mind, I gave her "miter". (discussed in the last chapter). While explaining its purpose, I induced a light trance by means of conversational induction.

I suggested that she hold her miter while going to sleep that night, and when she was a little drowsy, just like right now, to ask herself for a dream about ways that she could improve her situation.

She did this a few times, without much result except for feeling more refreshed and rested in the morning. But one night, she had a vivid dream, and she woke up to write down notes about it. So here's what she did.

They had several small lakes on the ranch, and they were full of Northern Pike, Bass, and pan fish. They also had horses. The house was big enough for several overnight guests, so Marge organized horseback camping and fishing trips for city dwellers.

Also, in cooperation with the local 4-H student's group, she hosted classes of students to visit the ranch and learn about real ranch life. (Ranchers don't like to see the younger generation go to the city, so that the land falls into corporate hands.)

She was a distant relative of the author Mari Sandoz, and was a fan of her novels of early settlement in the area. I suggested that she might carry on that tradition of writing, but apparently, she didn't act on that (as is usual with giving advice).

Marge began to again look forward to her mornings.

C. Teresa, What can I do?

Teresa was a 12-year-old girl from the Pine Ridge reservation. I was known on the reservation, because we cooperated with reservation human service agencies, and made referrals to each other when appropriate. I need to back up and explain about the people at Pine Ridge.

The Lakota, (Lakota are western Sioux, the other 3 branches being the Dakota and the Nakota) are trying very hard to preserve their traditional values, institutions, traditions, and religion. They tend to be distrustful of non-Indians (They usually don't mind that term, and many even find it amusing. They often call themselves "Indian people"). Some are hostile, and resent the presence of whites on the Rez. If you have ever been ignored by an Indian, you know that you have been well and truly ignored! They don't see you!

Teresa came in unannounced, to my office in a local church in a nearby town, and I made time for her. I could tell that she was brought up with traditional Lakota manners, she remained quiet and respectful, giving me control. I knew better than to ask her any direct questions, without first observing the system of preliminary courtesies. While talking, I found out that her uncle was the director of the reservation alcoholism program.

Eventually, I did ask her how I could be of help to her. She explained that her uncle wanted her to dance at the upcoming Sun Dance. As Director of the alcoholism treatment agency, and he would carve a stone Pipe for those who had gone through the 12 steps, and present it to them at a recognition ceremony. I once went to Pipestone, MN. To the park where Indians pilgrimage to gather the stone. It represents the blood of fallen warriors. It was a Sunday, with no one around, so I took a large piece. Whites are not permitted to do this, But I told myself it was for Roger. After I gave it to him, we were on good terms.

The Sun Dance is the most sacred of all Lakota ceremonies. The Lakota; and many other native peoples, believe that all things belong to the Creator, Wakan Tanka. (This is not a name, or a noun. It is 2 adjectives, translated as "Great Holy".

The reasoning for this is that- names are categories, and placing the creator in a category places artificial limits upon him. Compare this to the Hebrew tradition of not uttering the name of the creator.)

The Lakota; therefore, believe that the only meaningful sacrifice, or meaningful demonstration of devotion and commitment, is to sacrifice the only thing that is one's own, one's body. This is done in full view of the sun, the source of life.

You have probably seen pictures of the "piercing", where the men pierce their chests and insert pegs, which are tied to a tree. They then dance and pull until the pegs tear out of their flesh. There are other variations, but the point is- the sacrifice of pain. Sacrificing pain was also an old Roman Catholic tradition, and it still exists in some countries. The ceremony goes on for 4 days, culminating in the piercing. The men who do this bring great honor upon themselves. Young girls of Teresa's age also dance and sing, to lend encouragement.

I was well enough know among the Lakota to be able to attend Sun Dances. The ceremony is usually held at the village of Porcupine, just upstream from the site of the well known Wounded Knee massacre. This was the home of a famous Holy Man and author. I witnessed a man who was pierced on both his chest and his back, and tied to two horses. Then the Holy Man (Wichasha Wakan) whipped the horses. Another elderly man, with many scars from prior Sun Dances, had his back pierced and was tied to 12 buffalo skulls behind him in a line. The skulls were turned horns down, to dig into the dirt. Each time he would pull the skulls around the large Sun

Dance circle, his relatives would place one of his grandchildren on another one of the skulls, and he would continue until the pegs tore out of his back. He fell several times., but got back up by himself. I looked into his eyes as he was doing this, and there was the unmistakable "thousand-yard stare" of a deep trance. I also thought I saw an eerie light in his eyes, but that was probably just a reflection. I don't think that you can witness this without being awestruck and uplifted.

The only other white guy there was an anthropologist, in uniform with a baseball cap and baggage shorts. There is the story that the average Indian family consists of a man, two women, three children, a dog named Clementine, and the anthropologist.

So Teresa felt honored to be invited to dance, and felt obligated by tradition to do so, in obedience to her uncle. The problem came from her mother, a Christian.

Her mother had given up the traditional religion, and went to the Native American Church, which is non-denominational Protestant, while retaining many Indian traditions and ceremonies. ("Black Robes" are not popular on the Rez, but that's another story). Her mother did not wish her to dance in a Pagan ceremony. (the word pagan actually means "rural"). So Teresa was pulled from both sides, with no apparent resolution in sight.

I was aware that the Lakota believe in dreams. In fact, the solitary "Vision Quest" is a four day quest, for a dream of one's purpose in life. One does not speak of one's Vision Quest, but it is pictured symbolically on one's ceremonial shield.

So I took Teresa on a relaxation imagery trip, achieving light trance very readily. Indian people are culturally accustomed to conscious "lucid" dreaming, and take to hypnosis very naturally. They are dreamers, and they view whites as being somewhat backward, in that they have not yet learned to believe in the power of dreams.

I then offered the suggestion that she could dream about the part of her spirit that knew the best answer to her dilemma, the right thing to decide. She should simply relax, and let her spirit speak to her, whenever it is ready. I then said I had to go to the restroom, while she could dream in solitude.

I worked on charts for a few minutes, and when I returned, I saw her going out the door, and she turned, smiled, and waved.

I later saw her dancing and singing at the Sun Dance, and her mother was also there.

D. Group and Media Hypnotherapy

I was working at the Omaha reservation, helping to design
and build mental health services at the health center. I enjoy
being with Indian people. The Omaha are very congenial people.
They donated the land where the City of Omaha is now, in
exchange for protection from their ancient enemies, the Dakota,
to the north. The Omaha never were very numerous, numbering
about 5000 souls at the time. They gave land from their own
reservation to the Winnebago, and to the Ponca, when they
needed it. They never went to war with the whites.

I once did the progressive relaxation imagery with a group of
staff, and the Tribal Chairman was quite taken with it. He
referred his brother to me, for work on becoming a non-smoker.
Smoking The Pipe is a sacrament to Indians, used to help get
into the thoughtful, conciliatory trance. But recreational, addictive smoking is just seen as another bad habit.

Another health problem on the Rez is obesity and diabetes,
stemming from a diet that has become too rich in fats and in
alcohol, and these are associated with the yawning boredom and
isolation of reservation life. Alcohol was not allowed in public
buildings, even before that prohibition was "in".

So the Chairman had an idea to have a weight loss contest,
with prizes for teams that lost the most total weight. I should
mention that the abysmal poverty on the Rez has been somewhat

alleviated by the casino. Now; there are some jobs, family and health services, and poverty funds.

I was approached by some staff at the health center, to do some hypnosis for weight loss. So I began by teaching them to get into their mind-expanding trance, and that was very easy, they came to be able to do it at will.

While in our spiritual mode, I offered suggestions such as these:

"We can all remember the poor times in the past, when there was; often, not enough food. We learned as youngsters that it is good to eat fast, or you may not get enough food. These memories stay with us, even when we are not consciously thinking about them, and the habit of eating fast, and eating much, lingers. But if you direct yourself to eat slowly- more slowly,- you can stay in tune with your body, and you can hear it when it says to you- "that is enough". Relax and take your time when are enjoying food with your family or friends. This is a good time for you and for them, and it should be respected for its own value, and given the time that it deserves. You are able to eat as if you enjoy being an Omaha. And- you can remember this as you sit down."

"When you go to parties on weekends, you may drink alcohol. It does have a cheerful effect. And you may drink too much, so that you may act foolishly, and make a hangover.

Your body tries to get rid of too much alcohol, by washing it out with water. Your body then runs out of water, and you feel very poorly until you replace that healthy water.

And, your body can become so confused about what you did to it, that it can send confused signals to you- that you are hungry. It can mistake thirst for hunger. - But too much food can require even more water to digest. So then you may drink more beer. You are then caught in a whirlpool.

But you can get out of that whirlpool. Think about the taste of cool, clear water. How good it is, and how much your body loves it! You can listen to your mouth and your tongue when it is trying to ask you for water. Water is what the creator has provided to you. You can remember to place a glass of good water beside your bed, when you are going to drink alcohol. Your body will thank you in the morning, and speak to you clearly about what is good."

"Remember when you were a child.? You were thin and lithe and full of energy. So that life was a joyous adventure. If you listen to these words, you will be able to make your own ways to return to that joy."

"Food is also good. But when we eat fast, we may forget to truly taste it. We may swallow it in big pieces, without chewing it and tasting how good it is. We can save time this way, but we are missing out on the flavors that have been created for us."

We did not win first prize, but we did get a prize at the recognition ceremony.

Another idea of the Chairman was to travel around to the several Sacred sites on the Rez, where memorable historic and religious events took place, and where revered ancestors are buried; to film 360 degree vistas of the sites. There are places like Hole-in-Rock, the Sacred Fire Pit, and Blackbird Hill, and some places with ancient pictographs. The Holy Man, who I mentioned in the first pages of this book, was to go with me. I won't tell you where these places are, in order to avoid the inundation of tourists and litter. This video was for the old folks at the nursing home, who could no longer get to these places to meditate and dream.

I would read the progressive relaxation script (which I gave to you earlier) in the audio background of the video. They could go with me with that, or do their own meditating. Oliver would introduce the places, in the Omaha Language. There was talk of translating the whole thing into Omahan, but I don't know if that was in fact done. It was popular, and came to be shown regularly, and was duplicated for other groups.

148

Oliver was also the head of sanitation for the Tribe. One day I was walking by his office carrying a box, and he asked what I had there. I said "just some trash for the Sacred Dumpster".

He got a good laugh out of that.

I got a good laugh after I was rummaging through old tribal records to orient myself, and discovered that, in the original treaty allowing the railroad to be built, was a noteworthy clause. It agreed to the construction of the town of Walthill, to be used as a base for the construction workers. One clause stated that if liquor were ever sold in Walthill, the entire town would revert back to tribal ownership! (Walthill is now the primary source of alcohol on the Rez). So I ran over and showed it to the Chairman. He was already aware of it. He said- "Walt, if I ever tried to enforce that, they would find MY body beside the tracks".

One time Oliver and I were standing outside, smoking, and a man walked by and said something to him in Omahan. He just nodded his head. So I looked at him with a question mark over my head.

"He said that the Thunder Beings have come."

"What?"

"That, there, means that his daughter has come to her time of maturity. We will have the initiation ceremony on Saturday night, to welcome her into womanhood."

Such as that, is Indian humor.

E. Matt, the golfer.

I am not a golfer, but that doesn't prevent me from knowing about the basics of performance in any sport or game.

Matt was having trouble with his putting. He had been a pretty good putter, and he did not have any idea why his putting was now off. He hadn't made any changes in his style, in his equipment, or anything else that he could think of. I gave him an appointment right away, because it was the middle of the summer, and I had some free time in my schedule. I usually put a lower priority on non-crisis problems such as this, and kept a waiting list. I only worked 4 days a week, because I am one of those who needs the time to be away from peoples' problems, and to keep them out of my mind for awhile. You can get moody if you don't do that.

After trance induction, enough to set up the "contemplate" trance, I asked him to close his eyes, and picture himself on the green, at the last time he noticed the problem. I asked him to describe in detail, (with some coaxing for more detail, sights sounds, smells etc., to fill out his overall experience there, and to virtually take him back there). Then I asked him to go back to the tee, and describe that experience, also. He talked about the good cheer among his friends; they really enjoyed their golf outings, and they did a lot of horsing around together. Lots of laughter.

We then walked through each shot on the fairway, in the same way. I even heard the jokes that were told.

When we got to the green and he was preparing to putt, I asked him to switch into slow motion, so that we could take our time in exploring what happened.

He said that when he walked up to the ball, his friends became quiet. He said that they all did that, out of courtesy. During the long quiet as he addressed the ball, he said "Oh!, a picture of my fiancés face just popped into my head!" I asked him if that had any significance.

"She has an ugly frown on her face, as if she doesn't like me. We had a major disagreement about children, and things are pretty rocky. We have major different attitudes toward child rearing. I don't know what to do about it. I'm trying to think of some way to fix it."

There we had it. He was not only distracted during the quiet, but he was unconsciously tensing in his body, while trying to putt. His focus and his "muscle learning" were interrupted.

"Do you believe that you can solve the problem with her, on the golf course?"

He chuckled. "Of course not. (a little pun there, puns happen a lot with hypnosis). We can only solve it together!"

I then went into an Ericksonian monolog about how it would probably be OK, and not harmful to a thing, if he were to slip out of his concerned, worried mode on the course, just as he easily slips out of his serious- businessman mode and into his fun-loving mode, when he enters the clubhouse.

"Do you have other times and places to be concerned and worried; are you likely to run out of them?" Can you go off duty for awhile?" (Wait for the "yes"- no?)

I saw him again a couple of weeks later.

"That worked pretty well."

He and his fiancé had not yet resolved their disagreement; they were sort of ignoring the problem. So I gave him his "miter", and told him not to fuss about the disagreement unless he had his miter in his hand, and could imagine up for himself, an approach to working toward a solution.

F. Susan and the night terrors

Children can be both more challenging, and more responsive, in therapy, than adults. I suspect that they tend to be more responsive because they usually have not yet learned to distrust, and they don't tend to perform, play roles, or dissimulate. They can imagine and dream naturally. If you want to see a deep trance, watch a child in front of the TV, watching Sesame Street. If you try to speak to the child, she/he may actually not hear you at all. And, the child is likely to remember what they learn there.

With that, they tend to understand the world of dreams, and can be wa-ay ahead of their therapists. Six-year-old Susan was an example of both.

Susan would sometimes wake up screaming. She shook her head when her parents asked her if she had a bad dream, and would not discuss it, if they asked what the dream was about.

When I met with Susan, I therefore did not ask about bad dreams. The first order of business with children is to build some trust and friendship, without demanding anything.

"Sometimes you wake up being frightened, is that true?"

"Yes."

"Well, that is no fun. We should probably try to do something about that, don't you think?"

"Yes." (emphatically)

"I wonder if you have found a way to do something about that?"

"I go to sleep with mommy and daddy, right in between them."

"That sounds good. But what if they take you back to your own bed- what then?"

"I do the other thing."

"Would you tell me about the other thing?"

"Yes." (Nothing more. This literal response to the precise question is often called the "trance" response. The respondent answers exactly to the precise question, without any assumptions. Hypnotherapists know it to be an indicator of a deep trance. Notice that I did not even instruct her about how to do a trance. She intuitively knew what this place, and what this guy, is for. Notice also above, when I asked her about "I wonder"- she was not trancing, and she answered my-merely implied- question.)

"Please tell me about the other thing. "

"I build a house out of bricks, like the three little pigs."

I thought we had scored a touchdown here, but as she went to the door, she said: "the other thing doesn't sometimes work."

?

I called her back, and asked her what happens when it doesn't work?

"When I hear mommy and daddy fighting." "Please tell me about the fighting."

"Sometimes at night I wake up, and I hear thumping and bumping from their room, and sometimes mommy screams.

154

That's when I get up and go there, but they always take me back to my room. I'm not afraid for me, I'm afraid for mommy."

We had a Social Worker in the office who was very good at working with children and explaining things like this to them. I introduced them and explained the situation. The Social Worker couldn't help but smile.

G. Jorge, The Dynamic Executive.

Jorge was a mid-level executive with a national health insurance company. You should know that midlevel executives live; and die, by their ability to speak and command attention in meetings.

The decisions that erupt out of meetings in corporations, are largely functions of one's "presence" and also functions of the qualities of one's presentation of arguments. Jorge was referred to me by my neighborhood Mechanic, across the alley.

Going down the checklist, I asked Jorge if he had confidence in his ability to analyze problems. He replied with a confident "yes." He knew his field, which was Accounting and Finance. He said that he could indeed speak with expertise in his field, but that people would interrupt him, and drown him out of the discussion with the typical B.S., in meetings. He said that sometimes, in frustration, , he would say, "I am speaking here!" - to no avail to anyone.

His Simplistic statements such as "I know what the f**k I'm talking about!" were disregarded, and sometimes ridiculed.

I asked Jorge about dreams that he might have had.

"Yes! My wife complains about my tossing and turning at night"!

(OK- lets go with this).

(pause)

"My dreams are mostly about fights and struggles, with my monsters."

"Do you ever win?"

"No".

"Why not?"

"The monsters are white, and they always win."

" So let's imagine about something else. Maybe we could think about something else. "

" Can you think about a way that you can win"?

"No," I can't."

So let's back off and contemplate this "no- I can't" trance.

Jorge is telling us a great deal with this statement.

He is saying that, no matter how hard he tries, people put up roadblocks to his efforts to score points in meetings. He has thought deeply, and tried everything possible, with the same result.

He is also saying that he is not willing to explore ideas any more: "ideas" don't work at meetings. He is a martyr to ideas, and to a prejudiced world. He is locked into martyrdom, and is in no mood to give that up here. He will resist getting out of it. He may as well have said - "No, I won't."

So how shall we deal with such stiff resistance? He is an assertive man, and if I were to try being assertive with him, he would certainly be able to defeat me with a mixture of assertiveness and passive-aggressiveness.

One of Dr. Erickson's methods of dealing with resistance was to utilize the resistance in dealing with itself. He would encourage the resistance to a point where it became aware of itself, and/or it became laughably exaggerated. So I went into a conversational monolog trance (day-dreaming together).

"I am having a dream, I am having a fantasy". "If I did not have a dream, how could it come true?" (Confusion, again).

" I am a mouse in the corner, watching and hearing a meeting. I see a bright, capable, and assertive man struggling to achieve attention and respect. I also see a woman grimacing and rolling her eyes. I see a man slide back in his chair, and put his hands behind his neck. A couple of people are whispering together."

"Now I see the first man flushing in his face, and becoming

frustrated. He begins to speak faster, and more loudly. He appears a bit angry, and reaches for water for his dry mouth. His hands are trembling, and he begins pacing. He composes himself, and sits back down. The room is painfully quiet for a long moment."

"Now he is straightening his tie, and adjusting his jacket, as if he has come to a conclusion. He rubs his nose, and there appears on his face a pleasant expression. Another person begins speaking, and he leans forward in his chair, with his hands folded in front of him, and he is paying rapt attention to the other person.

As another person answers, he turns to that person with the same expression. He appears interested, thoughtful, and curious."

"Rather than trying harder, he is trying easier."

(Remember that we are day-dreaming, so we are speaking slowly, with lots of pauses for visual imagery).

"As he does this, I glance around to check out the other people in the room. I note some quick, furtive glances at the first man, and also some quick, furtive glances at each other. Something is different. He has not interrupted, and is not trying to gain the floor. The room slowly seems to become more relaxed, and more comfortable. I even begin to see a few tentative smiles."

(Count out)

"What do you think of the man I was watching?"

"He seems like a pushover, a loser. Only the strong can succeed in the boardroom. He is being naïve and silly."

"Sillier than what?"

Parenthetically, corporations spend time, money, and effort in trying to communicate to employees that cooperation is more desirable than competition., at least within our walls. Teamwork is hard to actually achieve, just by repeating the word often.

The next time I saw him, he said that he had tried the "loser trick"- -"trying easier."

"That's interesting- what happened?"

"Just as the meeting was wrapping up, the boss asked for my opinion!"

"You seem surprised."

"Yes, he's never done that before. And everyone; of course, listened to me."

This is certainly a major insight, and a step in the right direction, for Jorge. But before we declare victory for him, we need to remember that long-standing habits (trances) have a way of coming back, over time. His "strong/aggressive" trance is still likely to return at some time in the future. We really need to do something to implant and solidify this newer "respectful/courteous" trance, which is not yet strengthened by practice, over the passage of time. (Most hypnotherapists also recommend that clients return after a few months for a "tune-up").

I decided to reinforce this more adaptive behavior with a script that has been called the "Circle of Excellence."

"Let's do something that will help you to remember this; other, strength, that you have discovered. I will need you to stand up over here."

(We take a position in the middle of the floor, face to face. I place my right hand on his left shoulder, and hold his right hand in my left.)

"We are going to build your Circle of Excellence. Go ahead and slip into your calm, relaxed, day-dreaming, frame of mind. Simply, and easily, requires no effort."

"I'd like you to recall the last time that you were in a frustrating meeting. Recall the place... the faces... the voices... the mood. Experience it again with your mind's eye. Experience the feelings and emotions that float around the room."

"Take your time, and when your heart is able to re-experience these feelings, nod your head."

(Wait for the response. The longer it takes-the better. When he does it, press your right thumb gently into the hollow spot beside his neck, just above the collar bone.)

"Let's put that right here."

(The body/mind will record this. The left shoulder is closer to the heart.)

"Now... I would like you to imagine a circle of excellence-this is a place that you can go to, that makes it easy for you to know what to do. Build it as you like it; you can make out of gold, or crystal; you can color it, if you like. Make it yours. You have been there before, but this time make it so that you can see it. When it is built, place it on the floor in front of your feet."

(Glance at the floor, then renew eye contact. Even if his eyes are closed he will apperceive your glance.)

"Now, recall this last meeting, which was more satisfactory, in the same way. Re-experience the place... the faces... the voices... the mood. And when you have the feelings and emotions, feel free to step forward into your circle of excellence."

(Eventually, Jorge will step forward. As he does this, press the hollow near his neck again, while simultaneously; with your left thumb, pressing the hollow spot between the ring and middle fingers of his left hand, which you are holding.

"Let's put that here."

(The connection has been made in the body/mind. He will open his eyes, and smile slightly.)

"Isn't that interesting! ...The circle of excellence is yours, and it will appear before you whenever you need it or want it. It is yours. You can strengthen it be simply touching this spot, where it lives."

(Touch the spot between the fingers again.)

As he goes out the door, he is likely to be touching that spot. Notice that I did not count him out- he will remain in his excellent trance for some time. He will recall it; it will pop into his mind whenever it is appropriate, and it will eventually become automatic; not requiring conscious intent. Jorge came back for a tune-up again, about 6 months later. He seemed to me to be a happier, more cheerful, person.

Jorge responded to his frustrations at work, with aggression. That aggression could be considered as just grounds for dismissal, in some states. But many people respond in different ways to high levels of stress in the workplace. They substitute other ways of fleeing or fighting. Much of the time, people are actually unaware that they do these things as a way of dealing with stress; it is a form of trance.

Absenteeism

Turnover, job-hopping

Tardiness

Failure to communicate, secretiveness, withdrawal, negativity

Confusion, forgetfulness, daydreaming, inability to concentrate, procrastination

Inability to make decisions

Self-denigration, over compliance, "meeching"

Panic

General uncooperativeness

Fault finding, criticism, complaining

Playing "dumb"

Politics, power seeking

Sabotage

Rumors

Problem finding, crisis orientation

Feelings or expressions of persecution

Expressions of boredom and dissatisfaction

Apathy, withholding enthusiasm

There have been many studies into the expense of these workplace behaviors, and they are surprisingly costly.

H. Marcel, The Injured Running Back.

Marcel had a "hamstring" injury. This is a torn leg muscle, which is very painful and debilitating. It is serious, and requires the close attention of a physician and a physical therapist. It takes a long time to heal, and not only keeps the player out of the games, but prevents him from participating in practice. Further exercise slows healing, at best, and at worst causes further tissue damage. So even after fully recovering, the athlete returns being both out of practice, and out of shape.

I have heard physical therapists disagree about treating a hamstring. Some recommend heat, some cold, and some alternating the two. But they all know that temperature extremes, applied more than a couple or three times a day, can cause further tissue damage. (disagreement is necessary in all the healing arts; without disagreement, there can be no progress). The problem is congestion. The body tries to prevent infection in an injury by flooding the site with a wide variety of agents that are meant to prevent infection. But a hamstring does not involve a break in the skin, so the purpose of the congestion is unnecessary, and congestion can actually interfere with and slow healing, by slowing the full circulation of plenty of good, warm, nutritious, healing blood.

So Marcel and I decided to try a technique that works around the clock, without any danger of overdoing it.

Marcel's father was a freemason, and Marcel belonged to the young men's branch called De Molay. So I went down to the local Masonic store and got an inexpensive Masonic ring. You

have seen them, with a big "G", for God, a small diamond, and
the square and compass set in black onyx. (A ring won't get you
into a Masonic ceremony. You need secret words, gestures, and
especially a paid up dues card to get in there. The story goes that
a Mason and his wife; who belonged to Eastern Star, the ladies
branch, were on a plane over the pacific, when the pilot
announced that they needed to crash land in the sea, off of an
uncharted island. It would be some time before they were found
and rescued. The Mason asked "Did you pay the life insurance
premium?"

"No, dear, I'm sorry, I completely forgot."

"That's OK, did you pay our Lodge dues?"

"No, it slipped my mind."

He gave her a big kiss, and said "They'll find us.")

Anyway, Marcel and I went through the process of learning
(re-learning?) the trance response, and I offered him a lot of
suggestions and imagery about the healing blood

("And you can feel the warm, relaxing, healing blood,
flowing through the pain, bringing welcome relief and, bringing
healing to that part which is injured" etc. You can make up your
own suggestions and images. Then We did the glove anesthesia
script.

"I would like to speak with the part of Marcel that knows

about healing."

I got a signal from his ring finger, the one that I touched when I asked for a signal. I slipped the ring on that finger.

"I do not believe that this ring is magic. But then one can never be truly sure about much of anything. But if you wear it, it will remind you (the part of Marcel in charge of healing) to continue the warm, natural, wholesome healing, even when Marcel is not thinking about that. Marcel may return this ring if and when he wishes, but it's meanings will remain. And these words will be with you. Will you do that?"

Signal. Yes.

One thing remains.

With a hamstring, there is a tendency for the injured muscle to remain as sort of shy: to favor itself. It is as if, the muscle, its own self, is afraid of further injury. There is a bit of a "limp", or a hesitation.

"The muscle does, in fact, have its own mind and memory. The muscle does have its own memory."

"Nagging", will not help with that problem.

So we went back to the" shining marble library", and opened the book of "courage", which we know so well. We used the "glowing globe", with the power of the universe, to re-charge the muscle.

We might also, if his physician agrees, work on reducing the pain. Now, pain usually has a purpose.

That purpose is to protect one from further injury. Without pain, we might not adequately take care of an injury, or might not protect it. We can compose a monolog about how the sensation of pain, is a decision made by the brain, as it tries to protect you. Because it is a decision, it can really be called merely an opinion. We can ask to speak with that part of the brain, and persuade it to re-consider that opinion, in this case. I'll have more to say about that in the "non-smoking" discussion to come.

Another approach to focusing healing attention and imagery upon an injury, is to imagine the healing warmth and energy which exists throughout the body. As mentioned earlier, people tend to carry their normal everyday tensions in a specific part of their bodies. If you watch carefully, you can see that tension. It makes that part of the body appear somewhat stiff, inflexible, and perhaps a little awkward. If you remember videos of President Nixon, you can notice that he carried hi tensions and worries in his shoulders, so that it was awkward for him to move his two shoulders separately- they moved together, so that when he turned, he turned his whole upper body at once. Some of you may also remember Ed Sullivan, the variety show host, who had the same habit. Other people might carry the tension in their hips,

Their neck, their hands and arms, their legs, or their back. The place where the tension is carried, often carries a symbolic message, such as, "I am carrying the weight of the world on my shoulders", or "My hands want to change this, but the world won't let them"; or "What a pain in the neck".

I noticed that Marcel carried energy, and also tension, in his hips and upper legs. This seems logical for an athlete who's performance begins there. But the tension will hinder his flexibility there, so we will go for that.

"The energy that you carry in your hips, also brings with it tension. You can feel that energy and tension in your hips, can you not?" (Notice the use of the negative word, "not". The unconscious erases this word)

"You can, if you wish, gather up that tension and energy. It is warm, and carries with it some good energies. You can gather it into a golden ball with it's warm, healing energies, and you also place that golden ball somewhere else, where it may be needed, and put it to good use there."

"I suggest you place it in your stomach. You have been feeling some discomfort there, have you not? (People with strong anxiety often complain of stomach difficulties).

"Is it there?... that's good." Now, let's gather it up and move the golden ball of warmth and healing energy from your

168

stomach, and into your leg, which was (past tense) injured. Allow it to abide there, as you feel the warm energy focusing right where it is needed. And you can enjoy that for as long as you wish. Your leg likes it."

(Wait for motion, which will signal that he has finished the task.)

"OK- good. Let it stay there.

"I would like you to remind the golden ball of healing, from time to time. I would like you to do this again in the morning, before you get out of bed. Do it again after lunch-find a quiet place where you can lie down and won't be interrupted. And again just before you go to sleep at night. You will be able to remind the golden ball to remind you. As you practice this memory, you will become better and better at it."

"Will you do this?" (wait for a nod, no matter how long it might take).

"We can do this together. The muscle will regain itself. Can we not?"

Marcel was back "in pads", so quickly that his coach, his physicians, and his therapists, were surprised.

I. Nancy, The Non-Smoker

Recall Nancy and the "Pending Pendulum" from the last chapter.

There are a number of ways to focus the power of will upon unwanted habits and addictions. Each of these can achieve success, but more often, some combination of them is more effective. But, avoid overdoing it. There is a time to put a "period" on the end of the success sentence.

1. Breath and Breathing! (This script is especially effective if you have just shown your client some of those ugly pictures of smokers' lungs.)

"One of our strongest instincts is to breath. Nothing else creates more discomfort, so quickly, as an interruption of breathing; except perhaps fire."

"But enough of unpleasantness. The sensation of breathing is a great pleasure.

Smoking accentuates this sensation. In fact, the sensations involved in smoking are a large part of tobacco addiction; perhaps as strong of a part of addiction as is nicotine. (a slightly confusing sentence there.) Smoking sensations, like mouth, lips, lungs, eyes, (Here, smokers will remember the stinging eyes of tobacco smoke. Some hypnotherapists call this a "pre"-suggestion, which hints at an hypnotic suggestion, to come later.) chest, fingers, arm, and maybe taste.

170

Smoking tends to satisfy the breathing urge, and tends to reduce the amount, and also the depth, (another pre-suggestion) of breathing itself. And that results in a reduction of oxygen in the blood, and an increase in carbon dioxide and carbon monoxide! Then, you feel bad and get a headache."

"Just as smoking can reduce breathing, these good breathing habits (a breathing trance) can replace smoking."

"I suggest that you get into a comfortable position, so that you can easily go into your relaxation mode, and into your dreaming (or whatever word your client uses) - frame of mind. We are going to go to a nice place for awhile. If you feel like closing your eyes, that's fine."

"In your mind's eye, imagine that you are in an interesting and lovely hotel. Light, color, and interesting things are all around. Soft fabrics and plush carpets. There are pleasant things here. Enjoy. Before you is an escalator, going down. I wonder what is down there. So getting on the escalator, you go slowly down with it. As you go down, you will become even more relaxed and comfortable, without any effort at all. "

"Let's count all the comfort, on the way down. 10-9-8- 7- 6- 5 "you become even more relaxed" 4-3-2- and- one."

"Will you tell me what you see around you?" "Yes". (Again, a test for a deep trance. -A very precise and literal answer to my question).

"Please show it to me?"

"It's a swimming pool. People are lounging around, having drinks and talking. It is warm. There is a bar set up by the corner. I can smoke there." (Notice that Nancy has taken my job from me- she is doing her own trance.)

"So you feel the urge to smoke?"

"Yes."

"Keep that urge for a moment, while we ponder. I would like you to take a deep breath. Fill your lungs with the sweet, warm and moist, air. (smokers usually are somewhat de-hydrated, also). Savor it.- Now, let it go, slowly."

"Now take another, this time filling not only your lungs, but also your abdomen, with sweet, warm, moist air. Use your diaphragm to draw in more of it, into your lower chest.. You can have more."

"Let's do it again. It gets better."

"And again, just to be sure we can remember it." (at this point, Nancy is just a little bit dizzy, with her unaccustomed fresh supply of oxygen).

"Notice that your body, and your mind, feel grateful for the sensations that come with good air."

"Now I would like you to agree that, the part of Nancy that

knows about smoking, will remind her of this, whenever she feels the urge to smoke, and will remind her to breathe deeply and fully, 3 times, again. Will she do that?"

"Yes."

"And remember when we put the urge to smoke 'on hold'. What happened to that?"

"--It's not there anymore."

Alcohol is usually a "trigger" for smoking. They are both mouth-based automatic trances. We may want to do some more work with her, about re-associating alcohol with good, clean, air. Smoking is also a psychological signal to other people; a signal that says "I am comfortable with you, and I am willing to share my creature comforts with you." It is like "breaking bread" together. Perhaps we also need to look for other ways of signaling that same message, such as simple touching. More about that to come.

More- most people will describe alcohol as a social lubricant", making conversation and good cheer easier. But the physiological effects of alcohol are really such, that alcohol is a distancing influence.. It draws a curtain over true intimacy, and brings out the fantasy "roles" that we play for ourselves. "All the world's a stage", as the bard said. "Lookin' fer love in all the wrong places", as the cowboy sang. Alcohol-based intimacy is largely an illusion. Maybe we could attend to more direct ways of building satisfying relationships? For example, it is easy to suggest the idea that asking questions of another person, about themselves, is much more endearing than making statements about yourself. Talking about yourself seems like telling people how you expect them to like you. Suggestions; of course, are largely ignored, except when in a listening trance. Then, we can have a drink.

2. Re-framing. Words and Dreams Have Power. "Nancy, I would like if you would tell me some of the reasons why you smoke?"

Now, in the back room language of therapists, this is known as an "opening the flood gates" question. Go ahead and settle back, and let your client do the work. If your client is on a couch where they can't see you, you can do your grocery list. This is a popular approach among those who are being paid by the hour.

But seriously, folks.

The real purpose of this question is to encourage Nancy to get into her smoking trance. If she makes it all by herself, she will be experiencing it more deeply and fully, in her own words and in her own logic. When we get to the (upcoming) suggestion of an alternative, her self-induced smoking trance will draw alternatives to itself, like a magnet.

It just occurred to me, that hypnotherapy is all about alternatives. And with alternatives, comes freedom.

But anyway.

I had a bottle with a lid, that contained a rag and some gasoline. It was actually an empty bottle of martini olives.

"Smell this, and then say something."

"Yuck."

"Now go back, and remember when you first took a puff on a cigarette. That may be long ago, but you can remember your friends, and also remember the place, when you first tried tobacco. Take your time. When you remember, then say something."

"Yuck."

"So now I am going to offer some words to you. "Yuck" is one that I had not thought of. The words are "Bitter-Acrid". Please say that."

"Bitter-Acrid."

"Good. Are these words true for you?"

"Yes."

"Then, these words are worthy of your memory. Are they

not?" (Here, Nancy is a little confused about whether she should answer yes or no. But she is fairly certain that she would like to agree.)

"Perhaps it would be good, for that part of Nancy that knows about smoking, to remember these words. Do you remember these words?"

"Bitter-Acrid."

"You have some cigarettes in your purse. Yes?" "Right here."

"Take one of them out, sniff it, and then- say something."

"Yuck".

"Let's drink to that. Would you like to smoke to that?"

"No."

(She might say something like- "I'd rather not".) "Does your vaginal yeast agree to your decision?" "How did you know about that?"

"You and I, we command it to agree to stop itching. We have spoken together."

Sidebar- it is not at all unusual for us both, to apperceive things about our bodies while working together. Some of my clients have said things like- "go ahead to the men's room and pee.. I'll wait." We know this because we are tuned in,- together.

3. Lucid Dreaming.

"Nancy, I would like to speak about something called "lucid dreaming". That is-having a dream where you are aware that you are dreaming. You are also aware that you are able to direct and influence the story in the dream, and use it to speak with you about things that you are troubled about, or that you have questions about. Have you ever had a dream like that?"

"I think maybe I have, like when I wake up, but then decide to nap for a while longer. You get into a place like half asleep, half awake."

"Exactly. Would you like to go there again, now?" "Why not!"

"I really wanted you to say "yes." If you don't feel like it, or have somewhere you need to be, then we can do it next time?"

"No. that's fine. Let's do it now." (this is another pre-suggestion, hinting at what's to come, and also getting full commitment to it.)

(We are already in a light trance. Nancy is accustomed to trancing, and we have already begun to dream about dreaming. However, we need a deeper state in order to do this really well, so we need to go deeper. We can do this in any number of ways; by going to someplace or sometime where it is easy to be very relaxed but very aware.

We can go down an escalator, or to the beach, or to a mountain cabin, or to a special personal place that Nancy knows of. Then we explore the place, together, with dialog, all the while suggesting 'deeper and more relaxed', effortlessly.)

"This frees the mind to explore more freely, without being limited to the limits of the here and now."

(Trances can easily be deep enough, so that a person is so much into the experience, that they do not wish to speak any more. In that case, we can suggest that h/she simply come back to where they were when it was more comfortable to speak; and then to say "yes." After having done this, we can now go right into the imagery and suggestions.)

"There is a place in your mind where decisions are built. It is another mind within Nancy's mind, which is good at decisions. That place builds decisions, a piece at a time. It knows when a decision is complete

enough to move into, where we can move in, without looking back. These are firm decisions, made of bricks instead of straw, and the unmistakable feeling of real determination comes with them. It is like 'click', like a light switch, and you are confident that you have built a fully- decided and committed decision.

Have you ever used this place?"

"Oh yes- quite often! Well- maybe not all that often. Sometimes I hedge my bets."

"And that can also be a good thing. 'Maybe' is often a good idea."

(At this point- the phone rang! I switched to voice mail.)

"And you can easily ignore distractions, and go on without being disturbed."

"The pending pendulum has told us that your decision mind is ready to complete the building of a fresh new decision. Yet you have not yet completed the building of it. Since you have not yet become a nonsmoker, a free-breather, There must be some bricks which are not yet in place, or some kind of obstacle which is not yet resolved, which is allowing you to hesitate about a full, round, decision. Is that the case?"

(after a long pause).

"Yes."

(Here, Nancy knows what is not yet resolved. It came to her in another "click". But I am going to pretend that I don't know- that she knows. That will emphasize her own knowledge for her, and give her time to solidify that knowledge into her awareness. Whatever it may be, it is a new idea to her, and she needs some time to digest it.)

"As you wander through all the possible missing bricks, you may allow the determined part of your mind wander through all the possible lucid dreams, until it comes to an image that involves the missing brick. Things will come to you."

(Wait for some small motion, somewhere.) "Yes- good. Now expand that image into a whole scene, OK?. Please describe it".

(I don't need to test for deep trance by asking if she "will" describe it. I already know that she is deep enough.)

"We are sitting at a table, my boss and I, at my favorite sidewalk café."

"Because of all of my good work, I asked her for a new title and a modest raise, so we came to this confidential place to discuss it. After lunch and a glass of wine, she opened by telling me that she had already put me in for a 'small', -something less than modest', raise. But she had no other title for me. "Besides", she said, "a fancy-Nancy title would only make you more employable by someone else."

"I am nervous- afraid! This is my career! I am not experienced in hard bargaining! Decision time for me!"

(notice that she has switched to the present tense.) "So what then?"

"I needed time to think. I also needed to appear to be calm, relaxed, and to be thoughtful; and also to be in control. I reached for a cigarette and my gold lighter."

"OK-stop action. Lets pan the camera around so that it is behind your boss, looking at you. Tell me what you see."

(pause)

"I see someone who is nervous and afraid, and stalling for time. I see her with a crutch in her hands."

"Ok! In the game of poker, they call this a 'tell'. You have been read by her, and read by her accurately. No?"

"Yes."

"So let's rewind back to your ploy with the cigarette. What if, when you pause, lean forward on your elbows, fold your hands, simply make eye contact, and wait for her to say something more than what she has said, In your lucid dream, What then?"

"I see her leaning backward into her chair, with her arms folding, and saying to me- 'I'll see what I can do."

(Normally, I would try to avoid giving direct suggestions like this. It seems a little inelegant, and comes close to giving actual advice, which is so easy to resist. "Yeah-but". I would usually take her further into her own idea-making powers. But then, Nancy was clearly ready for this, in her very own lucid dream. Now, we can explore other times and places, where, and when, she uses the cigarette-reaching ploy.)

I think that it was Will Rogers, who said something like-
"Nobody remembers anything that they didn't discover for
themselves".

I asked her if her dream had actually happened, as in,- an
event that actually happened in history, before now.)

"No, but it will."

(One time I asked my grandpa, if his latest, old, story were
really true. He said: "Shorin' tis truth! Ye reckon nae ye'r weal,
lad?". Meaning- all of the possibilities are always with us,
waiting for us. The truth simply hasn't happened - yet, not yet.)

Later, I met Nancy, and asked her if we were successful. She
said:

"No. None of that worked. I had to do it myself."

(In all honesty, this last story happened with another client. I
included it in here, because it seems to fit so well with Nancy,
her own self.)

I chose the 'dreaming of the future' imagery for Nancy,
because she caught onto the trancing skill very quickly, and she
could do it easily and quickly. She was open to such possibilities.
Let me mention some other imagery that has shown to be
effective:

"I think we should discuss the things you have heard about

the difficulty of quitting. People can become brainwashed into expecting to have a great deal of difficulty, and into believing in "withdrawal symptoms, discomfort, irritability, and so forth. Tell me about what you expect?" (then, we can replace these fears with expectations involving words like 'fresh', 'clean', 'energy' 'breath', wonderful aromas', 'refreshing', etc.

Imagery about the relationship between parasites (worms, ticks, lice, leaches) and their hosts, as a metaphor for the relationship with smoking.

Similar relationship imagery about abusive relationships, with their mental and physical injury, and humiliation; and their habitual, repeating, and addictive nature.

A monolog about imagining what it would be like living under a dictatorship, vs. living free. This hit's a high note for immigrants.

A monolog about how discomfort, as well as pleasure, do not really have any material or substantive existence. These are really decisions that your brain makes, in trying to protect you from injury. As such, these feelings are really nothing more than opinions. And we can persuade that part of the brain that decides to feel a sense of deprivation, that the injury is in the smoke, not in the lack of it. And pleasure is not in the smoke, it is merely the appeasing of the part that has decided to feel the deprivation that really does not have any objective existence. So the decision to feel deprivation is not a fitting one, to this experience. We can replace the feeling bad decision with a feeling good decision. (actually, this part of the brain is called the nucleus accumbens, if your client likes intellectual stuff).

We can also visit our white marble library, and investigate the book of confidence.

We can visualize the cleansing of the tobacco related toxins from our blood and tissues, through our liver, kidneys, and bladder. We can smell it in the urine, and feel the freedom and cleanliness of its absence. Then we can connect smoke to this unpleasant odor.

We can investigate the "triggers" for reaching for a cigarette. The triggers are usually some form of actual or perceived social stress. These stimulus/response habits can be short-circuited by introducing another behavior.

"When you notice a trigger that is urging you to reach for a cigarette, you can thwart it by bringing your right thumb and forefinger together, which will remind you to use your deep breathing skill, and put the urge behind you."

Here is a simple trick that can be effective. Put a rubber

band on your left wrist, one that is just a little loose there. Then when you encounter a trigger, snap it against your wrist. This is a behavior modifying technique that, with repetition, will extinguish the smoking trigger. Use the rubber band with the "trigger" imagery above.

With well-practiced clients, we can take a trip into a moment in the future, to a time when we are enjoying being smoke-free, and free of craving, and free to choose. We can look back and recall how easy it was, after we had made a real commitment, and recall how we pushed through the brief uncomfortable moments.

As I mentioned, it often requires more than one type of imagery to achieve success. In my experience, only about 30% of successful clients achieved it in one session.

The range of possible imagery scripts is limited only by our imaginations.

J. Chemical Hypnosis

I once worked for a firm of private Psychiatrists. My duties included outpatient treatment, diagnostic testing, and making hospital rounds each day; with patients who were scheduled to see me on an out-patient basis after discharge from the hospital.

One day I was sitting at a table in the cafeteria with some of

Psychiatrist would be the overall manager of her treatment.

Now, Dr. Ryan was a very large, imposing, redheaded Irishman.

Myself and the patient got along well, and we did some good work together. In a few weeks she was ready to be discharged to outpatient therapy. I was standing outside the nursing station, explaining the medication that had been prescribed for her, and her appointment schedule, when Dr. Ryan walked up and said hi. She looked at him, looked at me, and back and forth rather frantically. I said:

"You remember Dr. Ryan?"

"Oh"- (hand to mouth). "I thought he was another hallucination!"

Anyway, back to Frank. He was referred to me for psychotherapy, with Dr. Burket, in our office, as the Psychiatrist in charge. As the new kid on the block, I was already accustomed to getting the most difficult and unrewarding cases in referral.

Frank and I got along well enough, but we were making no real progress. Routinely, with any of the varieties of depression, we begin by trying to understand the history of the patient. As Greg Iles, the mystery writer, said- "The past is never dead. It's not even past." Depression always has a long history of develop-

188

ment over decades, and every patient becomes depressed in their own way. The symptom of depression is the best way that the patient can come up with, to cope. When we understand it's development, then we can start to think about interventions and alternatives.

Frank did not remember any details from his life before he was about 15. He knew where he lived, and where he went to school, and some of his friends, but he had no memory of specific events or circumstances, except in very general terms. At the time, I had no training in hypnosis, so I was stuck in not having a clue about how to proceed. So I brought it up in our "group". Dr. Burket responded.

"My guess is there is trauma back there."

I responded: "I think so too. But how do we get at it?"

Have you ever heard of sodium pentothal?"

"Truth serum?. Isn't that for interrogating prisoners of war?"

"Yes, but it also has a way of getting around inhibitions, prohibitions, and repressions of unacceptable thoughts, and just might get around unacceptable memories. If you can do the interview, I can administer the drug". (This is all a paraphrase, based on the best of my memory.)

So we reserved an exam room at the hospital, and had it set

up for a regulated drip IV procedure. I spent a few evenings reading up, and preparing an interview strategy.

I had never done anything like this at all, and I was suffering some trepidation and anxiety about the whole thing. So the big day came. Dr. Burket signaled me that the patient was at the right dosage, and ready for the interview. (I will summarize the interview, to the best of my memory, with the most interesting parts. Frank's eyes are closed, but he is not asleep; He is in "twilight", as the Dentists say.)

"The other day, we were talking about how you were a very good student in high school, with excellent grades. Then when you were about 16, you started "goofing off", and your grades went way down. Can you tell me more about that?" (Notice that I am not speaking in the strange language of hypnosis; I hadn't learned it yet.)

"Yes. There didn't seem to be any point in putting out all that effort. No payoff. I found fun things to do. I worked and bought a car." (This later turned out to be a rationalization, an unconsciously contrived reason).

"OK- good. Now let your mind wander about that, and form a picture".

"I see my car, in the driveway where I bought it. I am counting out the money. Then I see my friends at the drive-in hamburger joint, looking it over. (pause). I am the center of attention!".

"Does that picture bring up another picture?" "Yes, this is before. I see the freshman football coach hollering at me."

"Why is he hollering?"

"I don't remember. He was always hollering at me, calling me names; ridiculing me. I tried very hard to please him, but it was never enough. I remember that then I hit the tackling dummy so hard that I broke it off its cable. Then I walked off the field, and I never came back."

"Why didn't you come back?"

"I don't know...I was afraid."

"Afraid of what?"

"I don't know."

"Had you ever done anything like that before."

"Yes. One night my mother was hollering at me about the way I was washing the dishes. She went on and on, telling me how stupid and awkward I was. She called me a 'son of a bitch'. Instead of looking at my feet and trying to look ashamed, I turned and laughed in her face. That's when my father came running into the kitchen. I ran out the back door and hid behind the church."

"What then?"

"He found me, slugged me, and dragged me back home. He

ordered me to take my bath, and go to bed. I stayed in the bathtub so long that the water got cold. I wouldn't come out, despite them hollering and banging on the door. They finally called my uncle, and he came over and took the door apart. He wanted to know what was wrong, but I wouldn't talk to him. I finally made it to bed."

"Did things like this happen very often."

"No. Dad usually just ignored me. So did mom, except when she could think of ways to ridicule me." (quiet tears).

"Do you have any good memories?"

"One. It has stuck in my mind. One day my friends and I were throwing a football around in the yard. My mother was standing on the porch, with her arms folded. My friends really didn't come into our yard much, and she was watching. The ball bounced up on the porch, and she threw it back to us. I'll never forget that... I can see it. Now I am back to the football coach... Oh! One time my grandfather took me fishing at their cabin in Minnesota. I lived with them at the time." (More quiet tears- I let Frank compose himself. He then went on in a loud, cracking voice.)

"They didn't like me! They hated me! And I hate them all!"

"The picture of your coach came back to you. What

happened after that."

"Nothing. It was never mentioned. I was getting big by then, and I started ignoring them all, and doing my own thing. I lived on the street for some time, and there was nothing they could do about it, except try to talk to me. I told them to f--k off!"

So Frank had encountered the hurt and humiliation in his past, that he had repressed; and also the hatred that he had used to deal with it. In therapy, Frank was now just a few sessions away from recognizing that his depression would keep on coming back to him as long as he harbored his rage. Therapists call it "anger-in", because it has a way of turning back in, upon oneself. Then, he would be able to recognize the blessings of gentle forgiveness, and re-join the human race.

In our "group", we agreed that there was probably more to the story. But as soon as Frank had worked past his rage and depression, he disappeared; so we'll probably never know the rest of the story.

You and I now know that we can accomplish breakthroughs like this with hypnotherapy, and avoid the inherent risks of powerful drugs and invasive medical procedures. And that's a good thing.

I feel like closing this chapter with a humorous story, and one has occurred to me. Let me lead into it.

Electroshock treatment (EST) is one of several ways to induce a grand mal seizure. Seizures seem to alleviate many of the symptoms of severe depression, even psychotic depression. It is used as a last resort, because it causes memory loss and confusion. Nobody knows exactly how it works, or how it works. With it, drugs are administered to prevent severe muscle spasms and resultant soreness, or even injury. Patients are almost always admitted to the hospital to do it, because of the risks, and the need for some recovery time.

Eleanor was scheduled for a course of ten EST's. She was; of course, nervous about it, and had many questions about what it was like. Dr. Ryan knew that she had a bit of a ribald streak in her personality, so he told her that it was like a "big orgasm".

Next morning she showed up for her first treatment, dressed in sheer lingerie and a sheer robe, and wearing very well prepared make-up.

194
Chapter IX

Using Your Mind for a Change?

Let me offer up a topic that I think is important, to just about everyone.

First, can you think of someone that you know, who is "bull-headed"? Someone who has rigid beliefs and attitudes, and who never changes his/her mind about them? I'd bet that you can think of a number of people like that.

Now, can you think of the last time that you changed your mind about something important? I'm not talking about selecting a shirt to wear today, or choosing a meal from the menu; I'm talking about changing your mind about one of your beliefs, attitudes, or conclusions. For example, have you ever changed your mind about politics?

Tough question, isn't it.

And now, think of the last time you tried to persuade

someone to change something they think, or something they do.
That one's easy, no? We must conclude that virtually all of our
communications with other people are really attempts to persuade
them about something.

And lastly, have you ever heard someone say to you
something like- "I never thought of it like that. I guess you're
right. I'm going to change my mind and agree with you"--? So,
are we just wasting our time trying to persuade each other about
things. Does our lack of success in being persuasive mean that
our words are just so much hot air?

I don't think so. As an educator, I cannot bear to think that I
was wasting my time in the classroom. And I cannot imagine
myself just stopping talking to people, out of frustration.

Fact is, people do change their minds. Not often, but they do.
They are just reluctant to do it in public. They don't like to get
caught at it. We would like to think that people (other people)
should change their minds more often, especially those who
disagree with us. When politicians change their minds, it's called
"waffling", and we tend not to give them much credit for being
flexible, or for discovering new information that changes their
conclusions or decisions. We might even say that the very
process of thinking is; at its heart, a process of coming to new
conclusions, which is changing one's mind. Learning; itself, is

also; and we don't tend to fault people for their learning's.

My own conclusion is- "Hoorah for mind changing and changers"! Every time we change our minds, we grow a little. Mind changing; I think, is a very mature thing to do. And I am not persuaded by the supposed implication that it means that we were stupid before. Let's be proud of changing and growing. None of us is yet finished with our task of building ourselves.

I have just changed my mind about the idea of mind-changing. Maybe I'll make a New Year's resolution to change my mind about something every day. To do that, I'll need to actively seek out new information, and I'll be learning.

Notice; in the above argument, that I gave you my evidence and my reasoning first; we walked through it together, arm in arm, and later we came to a similar conclusion. If I had given you my conclusion first, and then the logic and evidence, you probably wouldn't have heard the evidence.

Likely, you would have been too busy thinking about your argument to be able to refute my conclusion. My attempt at persuasion probably would have failed. Our conversation would have degenerated into "bar talk". Our habit is to first assert a truism, and then get ready for an argument. There is such a thing as "Friendly Persuasion", like in the song.

We tend to have another habit (trance) when we go about our
business of persuasion.

Political Scientists know that people have a strong tendency
to form a loyalty to a given political party. Traditional Freudian
theory says that this attitude probably came from a parent, or
another chosen role model, like maybe a boss or an athlete.
Then, that their loyalty tends to become cast in iron. Let me ask
you- when was the last time you paid any attention to a political
ad which came from a candidate of the other party? You
changed the channel, or went to the kitchen to build a sandwich;
right? If I had presented it that way, you might have folded this
book, turned off the light, and gone to sleep or something. We
do have a strong tendency to filter out the information that
doesn't support our iron-clad beliefs. As I mentioned before, this
tends to also set up the party line in academia, into concrete.
Isn't science supposed to be all about changing our minds? Same
thing with religion, but I don't want to get into that.

When we insist upon selling our conclusions, we set up a
competitive situation.

But when we ask questions or offer information that
stimulates reflection and pondering,- then- we have a chance of
stimulating some change and growth. This is why the

psychotherapeutic approach of Carl Rogers tends to be effective,
also. Some of his works are in the bibliography at the end, if you
like.

We might view hypnosis as merely a way to set up an
atmosphere of friendly persuasion, by way of reflection and
thoughtfulness, for a change.

Only mules and hand grenades are certain. "Maybe", the very
idea of it, is a way toward the future. "Also" can be another word
for freedom. There is honor in mind-changing, there is no shame
in it. Without a dream, how can a dream come true?

Next time that your debating opponent tries to buffalo you,
try saying something like- "I am thinking about something here".
See, then, what happens next. Try it, ok?

Alternatives are good, and we can make them, ourselves.
All of them.

In the last chapter, we met Jorge, the stubborn guy. We
stumbled upon a way to get past all of the stubbornness. We did
this by looking at himself from another point of view; an
alternative point of view. But that does not always work. There
are plenty of people who are set in their attitudes to the point that
they consider alternatives to be threatening. They seem to equate
alternative ideas with confusion, and even chaos. They do not

have the habit (trance) of being truly thoughtful and contemplative, and their conclusions put an end to further reflection. Contrary information , or the offering of alternatives, tends to make them resistant. Mentally, they cross their arms and tighten their belts.

The script that I offer below is another example of a "lucid dream", that we discussed earlier. I felt the need for another approach to deal with the "mind not-changing" trance.

Just before falling asleep, I asked my creative mind to come up with an inspiration about that. (Yes- it is a form of prayer. Prayers tend to work if you ask for things like courage, strength, understanding, etc. They don't tend to work so well if you ask for money or power.)

In the morning, while I was still in that half-asleep, half-awake mode, The outline of this approach came to me. Leave one of your minds open for the metaphors, if you want to be consciously aware of them. Also notice the many layers of abstraction, and time distortions.

First, we make a light, relaxing trance induction, by any of our methods.

(Again, use lots of pauses, to allow the imagination to run free. You can add more imagery and sensory detail, if you sense that the trance needs it.)

"Would you like to explore an interesting place?" "Sure".

"There is a monk that lives below the mountains. He is a mentor for the young monks in training. They come to him because he knows the way to get to Possibility Land. This land lies beyond the mountains, and the way is difficult and demanding, requiring both strength and courage. But the way, it is there."

"One day a young monk approached him, and after the greeting ceremonies, asked to be taken to Possibility Land. The old monk replied:"

'The way is difficult, but it is not dangerous. We will need to climb over Inspiration Mountain. We will travel through different terrains, and different climates, so you should be adaptable. You should dress sensibly. Wear layers of light clothing, so that you can be warm in the cold places, and take off layers in the warm places. Wear ankle length boots with good traction, because we will go through places with sharp rocks. A broad brimmed hat will protect you from too much sun, and from too much snow.'

"So the two of them set off in the morning sunrise. They climbed through many places; past rocks, snow, forest, and grass. Some were easy, and some were hard, but each was interesting and memorable. They reached the top of the mountain just as the sun peeked over it, and shown down on the other side. They continued down a slope, and came to a steep, high cliff, overlooking a green valley. The old monk said:

'This is the Land of Possibilities. Tell me what you see.'

'I see forests, farms, and pastures, with cattle, horses, and sheep roaming free together. Some of the horses can fly! There are deer, foxes, and rabbits. There is a river with boats. I see a shining city, with many parks and playgrounds, where people have gathered so as not to miss the morning. People and children are playing , and some are listening to speeches, and poetry. Some are carrying signs, with different ideas printed on them. There are vehicles flying through the air, and on raised rails. Can we go there?'

'Not from here. There is no way from here. We must return down the mountain and go another way. The only way is through the Cave of Certainty, through the mountain. The cave is really a dark tunnel, and it leads to Possibility Land. It has been there since before the memory of the grandfathers, and the people of Possibility Land could only have come there by going through the tunnel, as we shall. The tunnel is strange, dark, and frightening, with many demons there; but we must have courage and continue, or we will not reach Possibility Land. Remember that the demons cannot harm you, they can only frighten you.'

'But Master, why did we not go through the Cave of
Certainty in the first place?'

'I wanted to be sure that you really wanted to go to Possibility
Land. I wanted you to feel your sureness first!'

"So they returned down Inspiration Mountain, and prepared
to enter the cave at dusk. It was dark and damp, with many
passages. In one side passage, they found people sitting there, all
dressed alike, in dark robes with hoods. They were not moving.
They spoke only by giving orders, which no one obeyed. The
young monk asked:"

'Who are these people?'

'This is the Hall of the True Believers. The Gathering of
Absolute Certainty. Their Gospel is The Party Line. They do not
move, because they believe that moving around, implies that they
were in the wrong place to begin with. They rely on the Less
Faithful to bring them food. If we try to go past them, they will
move only to try to stop us from going to Possibility Land. But
remember that they have no real power over us; because they are
only bluffing and blustering.'

"So they continued on, into the Hall of the Tainted, where the
Less Faithful reside. These people were spending their spare time
by walking in circles, flailing on their bare backs with whips.
They were chanting ' Alternatives are chaos, alternatives are evil',

we must believe', over and over. They implored the old and the young monks to take up the whips, and punish themselves, because that is the way to the comfort and ease of sure belief. The young monk hesitated, and said:

'This frightens me. I'm not sure I want to go through there! What are they punishing themselves for?'

'Take heart and remember your goal. Their crime was to go forward and peak out of the cave, to get a glimpse of the Land of Possibilities. They are tainted by unauthorized alternatives, and they cannot be trusted by the System For Established Order again.'

"Then they went on to the Hall of Chaos. This hall is filled with naked people, running and jumping around, and doing anything that occurs to them, without restraint. The young monk was aghast, and asked:"

'What in the world is this?'

'These are the ones who believe nothing. They have rejected the ideas of belief and of trust altogether. The only order here is - if it feels good, do it. They are both overwhelmed by the Land of possibilities, and also repelled by the Cave of Certainty. They can neither go forward, nor go back. They are certain in their own cynicism. Come, the portal to the Land of Possibility is not far.'

"So they entered the Land of Possibilities, where it was already the next day. They were walking around the plaza, where people were visiting sidewalk shops, walking under the trees, playing in the fountain, dancing, eating, or just lying in the sun together."

"It looks like a Sunday afternoon!"

"Yes, but they don't name the days here. Naming our ideas has a way of eliminating all of the other possibilities. Names tend to build walls around possibilities, and as the Poet said-Something there is that hates a wall. They are free to work one day, and have the next day for play. So they enjoy both, and do not grow weary of either. Each day of work, they can choose from among the things that need to be done. They learn many skills. Come, here is a stall that sells excellent Scotch Whiskey. We can sit and contemplate together."

'They sell whiskey here?'

"Didn't you see the inscription on the Place of Worship?"

"All things in Moderation-, including Temperance."

"I noticed that you seemed to feel frightened and hesitant in the cave. Tell me how you dealt with that?"

"I just put one foot in front of the other."

So here, the child is father to the man. Now count out, with other suggestions, as you see fit. If your client is starting to feel overwhelmed, you will see motion, so that you can lighten up. Motion is a good sign, it says that your client wants to pause and digest what we have been doing.

Chapter X

Guided Imagery in Persuasion, Parenting,
Sales, Education, and Romance

In a way, the chapters so far have been leading up to this final chapter. It's probably true that most readers will never become involved in formal hypnosis, either as a practitioner or as a client. I expect that most readers are simply curious about it. So this chapter is for those who would like to become more persuasive in their daily lives.

As a matter of fact, most of our communications with other people are intended to influence them. We want them to change their mind about something, to change something in their behavior, to be aware of something that we are aware of, or to just think well of us, or like us. And we all know that all too often our attempts to influence are not very successful. We have discovered that most people do not change, very often at all.

This chapter talks about how we can get better at that. Listen up?

We have explored many of the simple principles of hypnosis and guided imagery. We now know that all change (albeit seldom) comes from the process of **imagination**, and the willingness to do imaginings. We know the power of contemplating possibilities, right? So- we need to focus upon how to encourage people to imagine and to contemplate. Most people only do that in solitude, and I don't think that time spent in solitude is ever wasted. But when we are with others, contemplation tends to turn into competitive debate. Can we get them to do imaginings with us? Yes we can.

If we become good at that, is that like mind control? No it's not. Not at all. It is a perfectly natural, and a completely voluntary thing to do. If you can get people to think about something in a way that they never have, they will enjoy it, and you will earn a reputation as a "good listener".

We like good speakers, but we love good listeners!

Persuasion.

Let's take a look at some of the most famous and persuasive

speeches in history. As before, I will place any of my own comments in parentheses. You might take note of the powerful ways that the speakers transport the listener or reader to other times, places, and events of the speakers choosing; and these times, places, and events carry with them powerful images and strong emotion, which the speaker wishes the audience to recall and to associate with him/her.

The Gettysburg Address- Lincoln.

"Four score and seven years ago, our forefathers brought forth on this continent a new nation, conceived in liberty and dedicated to the proposition..."

(Abe opens, and captures attention, right from the start. Virtually everyone in the audience will picture in their minds' eyes the well know portraits of Washington and Jefferson. They may even glance at the flag, and hear "...amber waves of grain".

"The brave men living and dead, who struggled here have consecrated it far above our poor power to add or detract."

(I can see the audience looking around the Gettysburg battlefield, and imagining.)

"... that we here highly resolve that these men shall not have died in vain... and that government of the people, by the people, and for the people shall not perish from the earth."

(Lincoln won the loyalty of America with this speech, and

But John skillfully took us from the here and now, all the way through the preposterous, into the land of the possible. He said "period", and "will be", to suspend our sense of the here and the now reality, in order to take us to a future reality. He took a large risk of being ridiculed, but there are many examples of his faith in imagination; his faith in the role of imagination in being a stimulus for inspiration. It's like another- "I have a dream".

And then look back to what happened.

Do you remember Walter Cronkite's- "We have a signal from the spacecraft!" And then the video of the triple parachutes?

The entire world cheered.

Granted, there may have been several other motives behind Kennedy's backing of this project, but we are still enjoying the medical, technological, mathematical, and theoretical spin-offs from the project.)

Winston Churchill, Message to the House of Commons, June 18th, 1940.

Background- In the early years of WWII, many European nations had sustained very many disastrous defeats. There was a widespread feeling in Britain that the nation should simply capitulate to the Axis powers, in order to escape complete destruction and massive bloodshed. Public opinion in the United States was strongly against becoming involved in what was seen as a purely European matter, but Churchill knew that help from the States was critical to Britain's survival.

Churchill began this long speech by presenting a detailed chronology of these defeats, in order to impress the House with the seriousness of the situation. Included here is just the last paragraph of the speech.

"I expect that the battle of Britain is about to begin... The whole fury and might of the enemy must very soon be turned on us. Hitler knows that he will have to break us in this island or lose the war. If we stand up to him, all Europe may be free and the life of the world may move forward into broad, sunlit uplands. But if we fail, then the whole world, including the United States, including all that we have known and cared for, will sink into the abyss of a new Dark Age made more sinister, and perhaps more protracted, by the lights of perverted science. Let us therefore brace ourselves to our duties, and so bear ourselves that, if the British Empire and it's Commonwealth should last for a thousand years, men will still say, "This was their finest hour".

(Churchill paints an effective picture of what will happen if Britain tries to appease Hitler, a mistake that his predecessor had already made. I think; however, there is some room for more engaging imagery. If he had shortened his exposition of all that had already happened, things that the audience was already fully aware of, then he would have had time to sharpen and expand upon the imagery about "sink into the abyss of a new Dark Age" and also "all we have known and cared for". These phrases need some images to lend them the fullness of attention and persuasion. I also think the image about "broad, sunlit uplands" needs some work. I like his choice of the term "break us", rather than "defeat us". Everyone gets defeated sometimes, but "break" is something you, yourself, must agree to.

Nevertheless, this speech did much to strengthen the resolve of Britain. It also influenced public opinion in the United States, and encouraged Pres. Roosevelt to begin providing supplies, materiel, and munitions to Britain.)

But enough about speeches. You can use these same image building techniques in everyday speaking, in order to engage attention and to encourage give-and-take discussion. All good therapists and conversationalists know that you get nowhere by telling people all about what they are wrong about. Check that! You actually get yourself into Rodney Dangerfield's shoes!- "I don't get no respect". You can instantly put a person in a defensiveness trance by asking - "Can you take a hint?"

Another snazzy approach to persuasion is called "Active Listening". There are so many books about it that I frankly don't remember who first used the term. I once prepared a lecture for my Management students, to give them an intro to it in a small package. So maybe I can summarize it for you.

Active listening is really an approach which sets up a positive mood and a positive relationship, wherein you will be heard, and also listened to, when you actually say something. It works well. Here are some of its benefits.

1. It gathers a lot of information about your partner, and stimulates further thought and explanation.

2. It helps to clarify your partners problems, and encourages h/her self-contemplation.

3. It helps to clarify the relative roles of information, logic, emotion, bias, and perception in your partner's formation of her/his attitudes. (Read that sentence again, it holds a lot.)

4. It stimulates new ideas, options, and alternatives. All change begins with imagination.

5. Builds personal trust.

Maybe a disadvantage is that it takes some time. Here are some of the techniques.

1. First, satisfy some of your partner's "talk hunger". I have

heard it called "thrilling" when my clients found someone willing to listen for a while. I recall a T-shirt that said:

"Obviously, you have mistaken me for someone who gives a shit". Ask open-ended questions that can't be answered with "yes" or "no", questions like- who?, what?, where?, when?, and most importantly, why? Ask for clarification. Avoid making statements or drawing conclusions.

2. Do not offer judgments or evaluations. Simply accept the words as they are. Do you have rubber stamps on your desk that say "valid", or "invalid?" Actually, I once had a boss who had a rubber stamp and a red ink pad that said "Bullshit". But that's another story.

3. Paraphrase. This is a good skill to cultivate. Carl Rogers pioneered "Client- Centered Therapy". You can get amazing videos from a local college that has a Human Services career line. It's basically pretty simple. You just think of other words to summarize , and to repeat back, what your partner has just said. "So you feel that your husband deserves to be killed?" Sometimes I'm surprised at how my clients can talk them own selves into being more rational and goal-directed. Even if you seriously disagree, A simple and noncommittal "uh-huh" or "I understand" is better. (Understanding does not imply agreement.)

A good question-, for when a therapist have been up all night at the hospital.- "Can you put that in different words?"

When I did a paper about the research in evaluation of psychotherapy techniques, Rogers got many of the "effectiveness" points. Also "client appeal" points.

3. Re-focus on feelings. Your client will likely appear with facts. (here's what the bastard did!) But their behavior will more likely be centered around their own emotional reactions. "How did that make you feel? Did he understand how you felt?" "How did he feel"? "I wonder why in the world he said that?" "What did you say then? Did it work?"

5. Please don't issue a challenge to a shouting match. If you want further contemplation, just raise your eyebrows.

6. Recognize and compliment genuine achievement. Your client will, with encouragement, be able to recall past successes in dealing with similar problems. Hear them, and recognize them. You don't need to say it. Your client will make the connection.

7. Nobody pays any attention to anything that they haven't discovered for themselves. That may be a harsh thought, but therapists know better than to preach.

8. With this foundation , you can ask very personal questions. "I don't rightly see other ideas. Do you?"

"You have grown, and you have grown by your own ability. I

think that you will continue to do that. I wonder how you will do that? I wonder how your next growth will come."

A topic related to active listening is body language, or non-verbal communication. This is the effort to read a person's feelings or attitudes, in order to gage how they are reacting to your words, and adjust your words and your approach accordingly. In Poker, patterns of gestures or expressions that may provide hints about what an opponent is up to, are called "tells".

Many of these gestures and expressions are automatic and involuntary, and are nearly universal among people. Others are specific to individuals, and you need to watch a person closely to pick up on his/her patterns of expression. Researchers report that anywhere between 60% and 80% of information about our intentions is received by others from our body language. There is a great deal of research out there about this topic, and I will try to summarize it for you. This short list is offered as a reference resource; I didn't write it as literature. Read it once, and then use it for reference and review.

But first, a word of caution. You can find quite a few books for sale that claim to be able to teach you how to spot lying. Almost every book about Poker will give you lots of advice about how to "tell" if someone is bluffing. As a matter of fact, most people will tell that they are very good at spotting lies, if you ask them.

Now, this book has lots of good news in it, but here I must bring you some bad news. Most research studies report that less than 2% of people can spot lies more consistently than flipping a coin. Further, if the trials are repeated with the same people, it will be a different 2% that spot lies well, the second time. 2% is about how many people will score better than chance in flipping coins! Also, Polygraphs (lie detectors), palm reading, and tea leaves are not permitted as evidence in court, for good statistical reason. They are simply not reliable. (Although many judges are convinced that they can read lies and remorse, as are jurors). So- unless you are certain that you are consistently in that 2%, please be very careful before you conclude that someone is lying. You can cause a great deal of injustice, and also mislead yourself. The best you can do is to look for signs that make you suspicious, so that you can investigate further. there are many accomplished liars out there, but even they are not good at identifying other liars. People get anxious and nervous for any number of reasons, and lying is just one of thousands of them.

What you can teach yourself to do is to spot signs of stress or anxiety, and also signs of confidence, comfort, aversion, and affection. All you need to do is be aware of some general trends in non-verbal gestures (given below), and practice your alertness to them. The more you watch for them, the better you will become at noticing them; and- the better listener you will become. Please read the last two sentences again.

Very briefly- Here are some goods signs to watch for:

Face-

The pupils of the eyes signal whether a person likes what they see or not. Pupils that get larger are the brains way of signaling that it wants to see more. The opposite is also true. Another signal is-- wide open eyes vs. squinting. Hands tend to move to the eyes when the eyes don't want to see something.

Frequent eye blinks are associated with stress or nervousness. Lowered eyebrows can signal that the person feels ineffectual, weak, or dominated. Employees who do that a lot are likely to quit.

Tight or pinched lips may signify aversion or strong disagreement, maybe even disgust.

It says that the person is trying hard to not say something unpleasant. Hands over the mouth say the same thing, but less emphatically. Any unusual mouth motion signifies that the person is choosing words carefully.

Beware of flaring nostrils! This is one of the ways that the brain prepares for action, for better breathing. Watch for this when you are on a dark lonely street at night. Also, any unusual eye motion can mean the same thing, or that the person wants to be elsewhere.

A tilted head can mean one of two things- either the person is comfortable with you, or are dubious about what you are saying. You can ask- "Am I making sense?". (Yeah-but... My dog expresses "yeah but-yeah but" very eloquently with body language). Either way, it signifies confidence.

Arms, torso, and neck-

The torso and neck contain vital organs, and the brain wants to try to protect them. When a person feels emotionally threatened, they will likely cover the torso or neck with hands, arms, clothing, or extraneous objects, such as the back of a chair. (false confidence). Even an unnecessary necktie can say that. Arms that show upward motion say that the person is happy, comfortable, and confident. If you watch game shows, notice that people express exuberance with their arms. Leaders and speakers do this. Don't vote for someone who grasps the lectern tightly and rigidly, unless you want someone who conceals their true feelings. Also, you often see very limp arms in the seriously depressed.

Restricted or contracted arms signify submission. Do this when you bring a peace offering home after an argument. Arms behind the back is a dismissive, segregating gesture. You don't want to see this when you walk into the bosses office. Hands on hips communicates authority, power, and dominance. Your mom did this. As a matter of fact, anything you do to take up more space also says this. Space = power. In a meeting, watch the boss stand and spread his/her arms wide and lean forward on the table. See that, and stop arguing immediately! Or, if you want to see who holds the real power in the office, watch the secretary spread "stuff" around her/his place at the table. When seated, leaning back with hands clasped behind the neck says the same thing.

Rubbing the neck is like a pacifier. It sends a signal to the brain to "calm down, take it easy". Same for rubbing pants legs and wringing hands. The base of the neck will usually redden, like a blush, when a women is angry. Back off. I don't know why men don't do this, except that men are perhaps less likely to conceal anger? Habitually angry people sometimes develop a rash below the clavicle. View that as their brain warning you to tread lightly. It's called "Helena's Collar".

Hands and feet-

224

Second only to speech, anthropologists will tell you that
hands, and the feet that allow upright walking and therefore allow
hands; are why humans dominate the Earth. So it's perhaps not
surprising that our brains view them as highly important, and use
them for self-expression. Well trained mail carriers know that
dogs express themselves with teeth. When you see a dogs teeth,
you should "tell" your peaceful intentions by hiding the human
weapons that dogs fear most-your hands and feet. Sit on your
heels, and extend one fist so the dog can safely sniff out your
emotional status. (it's the fingers that they fear).

If you are acceptable, the tail will tell you so. If not, withdraw
your fist and slowly rise and back away.

At that, that dog will "snuff" (expelling your unacceptable
scent) and turn its head to the side, granting permission for you to
withdraw. Rest assured that normal dogs are very aware that, if
they actually get violent, things will go from bad to worse very,
very, quickly. They want peace with security. Only extreme fear,
loyalty, or Rabies will lead them to actual violence against
humans. They enjoy barking at mail carriers simply because they
always win. The mail carrier always goes away. Likewise with
chasing cars and chasing lawn mowers.

But back to the point.

Among people, fists are warnings, signs of hostility. Open palms and handshakes are requests for peace, and signals that "I will not draw a weapon". In Europe, they rode on the left side of the road so that their sword arm was exposed. In the West, the pistol was drawn from the right.

In conversation, I'd recommend that you keep your hands visible, on the table. To the brain, concealed hands = concealed motives. Also, don't use your index finger to point., especially not directly at a person. Point at yourself in a mirror, and you'll sense the threat even from yourself. If you must point, for instance when you are a speaker taking questions, point with your index finger and your middle finger side by side. This removes the implied threat.

Avoid playing with your hair, or preening, unless there is some degree of intimacy between you. Preening is a signal of dismissal., or disrespect.

If you want to exude confidence, "steeple" your hands, with the tips of your fingers touching. This also sends a signal of thoughtfulness and sincerity. A more subtle sign of confidence is holding your hands so that "thumbs are up". Low confidence is communicated by lack of motion in hands or arms, or withdrawing (contractor) motions.

Under the table, concealed feet = a wish to be elsewhere.

Crossed ankles = insecurity. Feet generally point in the direction that they wish to go, usually away. If a person's feet point toward you, it's a signal that they wish to continue the conversation.

Jiggling feet indicate the wish for the rhythm enjoyed in the security of the heartbeat of the mother's womb.

We have heard of the term "foot fetish". I tend to understand this as an old, atavistic memory of the time, when anthropoids could tell about the reproductive status of a female, from the scent of her footprints. Same with panties.

We all see the sign of twirling the index finger; back to front, down and back, and up, in a twirling motion. This means "Bear with me, I am trying to build up to a point". It usually indicates sincerity. But-it can be faked, as can all of these gestures.

Shoes also tell a story. Noisy shoes say "I am noisy". High heels say "I have a nice butt! Athletic shoes say -"I am energetic". Polished shoes say "I am fastidious". Loafers say, "I will make up my mind later maybe". (flexible).

But enough- if you want more on this topic, there are plenty of books and videos.

Parenting

Many people feel that our relationship with our children is at least as important as our career relationships, and more important than our social relationships. (As people grow older after their 'teens, they tend to see romantic relationships as less important).

Before I begin here, I want to express a strong conclusion that I came to after many years as a university educator. I have debated this with many educators, from pre-school on. As we move up in the grades, they tend to agree with me more and more.

Since Benjamin Spock wrote his famous book, our public schools have largely switched from seeing education as acquiring learning and discipline, to seeing education as a vehicle for inculcating "self- esteem".

Now, I have nothing against self-esteem. I have seen too much misery that can be traced to low self-esteem. It's just that I have concluded that it should be earned, rather than given as a birthright. "Self-esteem" in education now seems to assume that if a child has high self-esteem, they will somehow achieve more.

This idea has the cause/effect relationship backwards! Achievement causes (real) self-esteem; self-esteem does not cause achievement! Self-esteem without achievement; first, is mere complacency! Complacency! Real self-esteem comes After work. Our kids seem to be in a self-esteem, self-love trance! And it is not a productive one.

This idea that "God loves me, no matter what", is insidious. God, by any of His many names, appears to have a set of very strict rules about whom He finds acceptable.

I have seen the results in college. Every year, we needed to "dummy-down" the curriculum, because fewer and fewer students are willing to actually make effort. Many seem to feel that education is the teacher's job, not theirs. It's what the teacher does, certainly not what they do. Many refuse to even read the book, and will sue you if you try to fail them. We see fewer foreign students, because an American degree no longer has the status that it once did.

But maybe I've gone past curmudgeon, nearly all the way to "fogy".

Earlier in this book we talked about experimental rats in the laboratory. We came to the conclusion that positive reinforcement (reward) shapes behavior much more effectively than does punishment. Now let's take this a step further, to parenting. We will need to make some adjustments to our conclusions about rats, because children (at least after age 5-7 or so), discover this thing called "meaning".

Rats readily learn to change and adapt their behavior based upon the apparent results of that behavior. (As a matter of fact, so do all living organisms, including plants!). Rats have learned to adapt to all the different environments on earth, except underwater and perhaps Antarctica. Children also learn from reinforcement, and tend to repeat behaviors that are associated with desired outcomes. "Desired outcomes" include, very importantly, approval and affection from parents. Post-infancy children can even begin to progressively understand punishment; they eventually come to be able to carry on abstract reasoning- something like "Maybe they frown at me because they don't want me to do that". On the other hand, behavior that changes because of reinforcement does not require reasoning, it is automatic and unconscious.

There is also something called negative reinforcement. This is nether reward for desired behavior, nor punishment for undesired behavior. It is simply the withdrawal of reward as a consequence of undesired behavior. For humans who are capable of reasoning, it can be even more effective than reward. Let me give you an example.

My grandson once climbed into his parents' SUV. He must have memorized the sequence: he started it, stepped on the brake to release the gearshift, dropped it into reverse, and backed into a tree (yes, there was damage). He was about 4 1/2.

Now, the normal reaction of parents to this would be extreme agitation and anger, no? Grounds for grounding. But, his parents simply took him from the car, avoided any eye contact or facial expression, put him aside, and inspected the damage to the car and tree. The boy just stood there, looking sheepisher and sheepisher. Nothing was said to him. They merely withdrew their affection, temporarily.

But he got the message loud and clear; he never did anything like that again.

Here's the trick to all this. If you use primarily punishment to teach your child, this will make your relationship with the child a primarily negative one. Generally unpleasant.

If you use at least an equal amount of reinforcement and reward (affection), then the relationship will be generally positive, and the child will value the relationship, and try to preserve the relationship. That's important, you don't want the child to reject the relationship. It's a matter of balance, like the balance scale that you see in the hands of "Justice" in a courtroom.

In addition, whatever learning which comes from punishment tends to be temporary, and is specific to the punisher. If the punisher is absent, then so is the learning. That's why so many drivers forget traffic laws when they don't see a cop. Please don't spank your child for running into the street unless you can be there at all times! Forced compliance is only enforced when the force is there. Teach them, rather, the procedure for safe street crossing, and recognize and praise their achievement when they do it.

Another good idea. When you must apply punishment, be sure to explain what it is that you are punishing, explain why in terms of the "normal and natural consequences" of the behavior, and suggest and reward other alternative behaviors. Do this before applying the punishment, because punishment stimulates all kinds of powerful emotions in children, and these powerful emotions block out any possibility of any learning. Panic is incompatible with intellectual activity. It also allows you to count to ten.

Another- use your skills in "active listening" (presented above) in your conversations, especially with children. It teaches them mutual respect. You may remember the "golden Secret", discussed earlier, about setting up a rational and reasonable trance relationship.

Another- Remember the "Pygmalion Effect", wherein people tend to become what you expect of them? Try to avoid any ridicule or humiliation, OK?

Let's do a one question quiz, OK?

There is a lot of research about the "best" answer to this

question, but the results of parenting skills do lack a very much research into the many thousands of possible outcomes of parenting methods, and the very long term results over the child's entire life. For that reason, the "best" answer is still largely a matter of opinion.

Feel free to disagree with me.

So Here's the question:

In your opinion, what is the most important factor in parenting?

a. Consistent rules.

b. Strict rules.

c. Enforced authority.

d. Instilling self-esteem.

e. a good relationship.

Here's my response to the question.

a. Consistency is nice, but I don't think you are doing your child any favors by teaching them to expect consistency in the world. They will have lots of teachers, bosses, organization, and friends who are inconsistent. Live with it.

b. I think that flexibility is a higher value than strictness. When situations are different, one from the other, then I think we should recognize that. Let the child explain, and then respond.

c. I already explained why I don't expect much in the way

d. Ditto for self-esteem without, first, achievement.

e. This is my favorite answer.

If your relationship with your child is marked by Thoughtfulness, Respect, Affection, and Courtesy (the "TRAC" trance), then the child will respond likewise, will value and preserve the relationship, and will carry this trance into life h/her life.

Make no mistake, children are very acutely aware of whether you *like* them or not. You can do your "I like you" trance. Picture your favorite family sit-com.

<u>Unconscious components of a decision to buy.</u>

Perhaps the branch, or sister, of hypnosis that offers the best help with sales is Neuro-Linguistic Programming, or NLP. It was first introduced by Richard Bandler and John Grinder, but there has been much more literature and research lately, inspired by their books. They studied outstanding achievers in the human sciences, and distilled their methods into a conceptual summary. One of the people they studied was Milton Erickson, to whom this book is dedicated. In fact, when asked about NLP, Dr. Erickson observed-"Yes. I do that; also".

My own application of it, to sales, rests on my assumption

that a decision to buy is a complex thing, involving several
modalities of thinking, and that a decision to buy requires a
commonality, or congruence, among these modalities of
thinking.

I see a sales person not as a persuader, but as a decision
consultant, guiding the costumer through the difficult decision
process, based on keen observation of the customers mannerisms
and words. Failure to do this usually results in "Let me think
about it"; which is a clear no!

Doing it very well does not guarantee a sale, but it does up
the odds. It does make for a good decision, without "buyer's
remorse".

Before I explain that, I will need to explain some
fundamentals of decision building (Not decision "making"). In
the back of their minds, people have goals that they wish to
achieve by means of a decision. These goals are both intellectual
and emotional. But most people will find it difficult to tell you
about their wishes, mainly because they have not yet put their
wishes into words, even to themselves. So the goals/ wishes still
remain unconscious to them.

I will explain by paraphrasing Maslow's "Hierarchy of
needs", which is still a subject of ongoing research and
modification. A basic tenet is that people's needs and wishes

change over time. As one need becomes satisfied, their attention shifts to another need. The progression from one need to another has been shown to be largely predictable. Here is the typical progression. For sales purposes, we need to become aware of which needs a person is seeking to satisfy with a purchase decision. For illustration, let's use the decision of buying a car as an example.

A. Basic biological needs come first; food, clothing, and shelter. For our purposes here, we can ignore this level, because a person who is cold and hungry is not likely to buy anything else.

B. Safety and security. When a person is reasonably bodily comfortable right now, attention shifts to building decisions about security and comfort in the future. This person wants to know how your product can contribute to that feeling of security, From this person you will hear words that have to do with fear, anxiety, or insecurity. (e.g. disappointed, discouraged, regretful, resigned, slighted, deprived, disturbed, etc.), It's a good idea to respond with words that have to do with confidence and safety. (valued, gratified, assured, relieved, grateful). People at this stage have a conservative bias, and need some personal hand-holding before they will be able to move on, up the needs hierarchy.

C. Social needs. When a person feels reasonably safe and

secure, attention shifts to building decisions about other people., and to the social process of fitting in with a particular reference group(s). This person is thinking about how they can be of value to his/her peers, or to her/his own customers. They will speak about values and about questions of social behavior and expectations (fashion?), and they will use a lot of pronouns (he, she, they, them, us.) They like to communicate about value or goodness. Your best response here is active listening, ask them open-ended questions about the important people and groups in their lives. Encourage them to explain their social situation and how they think about and understand the various people and groups that they deal with. Paraphrase; repeat what they tell you in different words. Encourage a "verbal enema". Do not inflict any positive advice; they will respond to advice in the negative. You will likely be surprised at the amount of personal information that they will enthusiastically share with you, and this information will guide you to their "hot buttons".

D. Status and esteem needs. When a person begins to feel reasonably competent and secure in their own social value, their attention begins to shift to personal decisions about 2 kinds of status and esteem:

1. Status and comparative positions in groups, and
2. Self-esteem; their underlying and personal feelings of self

respect and self approval.

These people want to go beyond A, B, and C above. They want to make a statement about themselves and about the respect that they deserve. At the extreme, people at this phase can get into a "ME" trance. They want to become convinced about how your product can contribute to their image. Your product should also serve as a symbol of their social success and their position among their peers. They can accept advice if they see your product as having achieved status relevant to its competition, and see you, yourself, as successful. If you sell status symbols, dress for the part. Their words will have to do with progress and advancement, rather than about protection or about avoiding negative things.

From these people, you will hear words like excited, enthusiastic, resolved, encouraged, optimistic, proud, assured, determined, confident. They will be assertive, and you should match the assertiveness; but also avoid open competition and one-upmanship. Focus on them. You can out-do their courtesy and politeness if you like. Go ahead and tell them your story; go ahead and sell yourself. There is an opportunity to close, if you can help them up to this level. These people want to take action.

E. Self-actualization needs. When a person has reasonably satisfied all of the above needs (or at least has explored, discussed, or thought about them in a positive way), their interest shifts to matters of personal growth and development. They want to learn, to be all they can be, and to actually realize all the potential abilities that they have. They often wear clothing that signifies what kind of self-improvement they are working on at present, for example athletic shoes or organization symbols. They speak of the future, and they often use the subjunctive (perhaps, maybe, if). Your product is of additional interest to them if it helps them become somehow more than they are right now. These people are able to talk about their weaknesses and shortcomings, and they have the confidence to fantasize out loud about what their personal aspirations and goals are. Encourage that. Show them your own personality; they are curious.

Don't be afraid of silence- these people are thoughtful, they will build their decision in a moment of silent reflection, not in the midst of conversation. They want to become more able, and they will be interested in after-market follow up and consultation. Their general goal is achievement. Who can I become? How will your product contribute to that? They will use words like energized, uplifted, gratified, admired, fulfilled, good, pleased, proud.

These are willing and able to close if you truly have a good product. They are not idle shoppers; they spent some time in building a decision to talk with you. As a salesman, you hope that you are lucky enough to see a lot of them. You might decide to direct your advertising toward them.

As a Decision Consultant, your job is to help people along in the progression and development of need satisfaction. Make contact with them at the level of need that they come with, take their hand, and lead them up the progression at their own pace. When they use negative words, offer them positive words to replace those. But, bear in mind that few will reach the self-actualization level.

With that, now let's speak about neuro-linguistic programming, as I promised. A basic observation from NLP is that there are actually 3 different languages that we use to think with, and to build decisions with. The languages are called Auditory, Visual, and Kinesthetic.

Just about everyone is able to use all 3, but most of us have a favorite which we like to use first. Before I explain them, let me make a main point. A positive decision to buy requires the attainment of comfort in all 3 languages! Without all three, the decision is "Let me think about it", or , if a sale is made, buyer's remorse is a result.

Your job as a Decision Consultant is to make contact in the

person's presenting language, and then to lead them through the other two, so that a comfortable decision becomes possible. A comfortable decision is yes or no, the uncomfortable one is "Let me think about it". If you can get a clear yes or no, then you have done your job well. The law of averages will then treat you well.

A. The Auditory language. This style involves thinking in words and in logic. The person who likes this style will present by talking about cost, benefits, service, warranties, and other logical and concrete things. For example, a car buyer may begin by questioning price, mileage, service record, reliability, etc. This person wants you to respond with clear, direct answers and supporting evidence. Do not change the subject until you feel they have comfort in this area. This person is a comparison shopper, and will want the information to make a fair comparison. Linger with them and answer questions with confidence and fairness. Don't push. If you have the courage to say something like

"Ya know, it might be worthwhile for you to check out the competitive car down the street!", you are likely to see this person again.

A. The Visual language. This style involves thinking in pictures, or images. You do this when you plan your route to go somewhere. You don't do that in words, you do it with very rapid pictures of the route in your mind, and of where you need to turn. Think about going to the grocery store? The person who likes to think first in pictures will use words like look, see, understand, imagine, picture, pretty, watch, appear, etc. This person wants to be comfortable with how the decision will appear, to the important people in h/her life, as well as to themselves. For example, a car buyer in this mode will want to imagine how it will look in the driveway and to the neighbors. Help them do that. They often stand back to get a better view. (either actually or verbally). In fact, most of us have a person in our lives whose opinion of our decisions is important to us. There is also a picture of that person in the back of our minds. If you can find and talk about that person with your customer, then you have accomplished a piece of art.

C. The Kinesthetic Language. This style involves thinking in feelings, emotions, sensations, and intuitions. This person wants to explore how it will feel to use your product, and how it will feel to *decide* to use your product. They feel good about a decision, or not. This is by far the fastest of the three languages. This is the one your brain uses to ride a bicycle, for instance. Imagine what it would be like to ride a bicycle but giving word instructions to all your muscles, tuning them to the precise right tension, and doing that instantaneously, and changing the instructions instantaneously. No computer can do that! But you can do it, while simultaneously thinking about your job or something. And you cannot learn it in a book of words (auditory), it is not enough to visualize it, you must develop a feel for it.

First impressions are important to this person, and those impressions are not necessarily logical. When these persons express an opinion, they often say "I feel", rather than "I think". They will want to touch your product, and try it out.

Here is a very useful piece of knowledge! A person's eyes will tell you which language of thought they are using at a given moment. Without realizing it, people make very rapid motions with their eyes that signal the language they are accessing. You can watch for those rapid movements.

Picture someone's eye, looking out at you. While you're at it, you might as well make it one of those smiley faces.

A quick glance up ant to the right (your left), is visual mode. It is also "constructed", in the sense that the person is imagining what something might look like. A glance up and to the left is also visual, but recalled; they are remembering something they actually have seen.

A glance sideways to the right is auditory; words. To the

right is constructed thoughts, and to the left is actual words being remembered, or that have been thought before.

A glance down and to the right is kinesthetic. Feelings and intuitions are being consulted.

There is conflicting research on the unusual quick glance down and to the left. Apparently it has something to do with sound. It's unusual in people who are not musicians. A quick glance straight down means "I think I'll stop talking now".

Watch your customers eyes for these quick glances. Talking involves rapid decision making about what to say. So their eye movements give clues about how they habitually arrange their thinking while making decisions. If one of the languages of thought is missing in that process, guide them toward that modality. The kinesthetic mode is often the one that is missing. Ask something like- "How do you feel about that"; or "what does your intuition tell you?".

To repeat, a comfortable decision requires achieving comfort in all three modes. You can help your customer reach a decision by making initial contact in their favorite, or first, mode; and then leading them through the other two, at their own pace. As a Decision Consultant, your goal should be a clear yes or no, rather than always a yes. You'll get some of each.

So we have 3 decision building languages, and 4 levels of motivation, for a total of 12 different categories of customers.

You may have heard the story of a visitor to New York who asked a person on the street: "How can I get to Carnegie Hall?"

"Practice--Practice".

As you practice this and gain experience, you will become able to make contact and guide your costumers to a good, comfortable decision. It will become easily and effortlessly automatic for you.

<u>Hypnosis in Teaching</u>

It has probably become clear to you that everyone uses hypnotic principles when they are trying to be influential with other people.

It's just that some are more skillful with it than others.

But hypnosis is almost never used in public schools! (at least it is not labeled as such.) I imagine that is because some parents would surely object. Parents words are always heard in public schools, whether they are well informed, or not.

Ralph Dale has written on article on this topic, and I think it is well done, and also courageous. (U.S. Dept. of Education, ERIC #ED087710.) In it, he cites 9 uses of hypnotic principles in teaching. In summary:

a. reinforce positive habits, and to relinquish negative ones

b. expand consciousness by increasing sensory and sensual response

c. improve concentration

d. improve motivation

e. aid memory

f. diminish mental blocks

g. reduce anxiety

h. encourage original thinking

i. develop self confidence.

Regarding g. above, I used to routinely do the relaxation exercise in chapter 3 for my Statistics students. The Statistics course is required for nearly all college students now, and it inspires many students with anxiety and trepidation, because it has a reputation for being very difficult, and for being a grade average buster. In general, Statistics is mathematics applied to decision building. Test anxiety is a very disabling condition, and that is especially true in Statistics. It's not immodest to point out that my Statistics classes always filled first.

The "Case Method" is a structured teaching technique which was apparently first developed at Harvard Business School. It is now widely used in many Business Colleges, and also Public

Policy schools. There are mountains of published cases offered to be used in teaching, and many teachers write them to score publications in order to make rank. (Publish or Perish!) It can be used in any topical field that requires decision building.

It goes like this. It begins: of course with the assumption that the participants have actually read the textbook. Generally, students get a copy of the case well before class, so they can ponder it. A decision problem is presented, with any needed background information. The cases are real- they really happened. But there is no clearly correct answer. Roles are often assigned to students, representing the various functional executives whose viewpoints should be involved in the decision process.

The debate becomes quite fast and furious. If you were a mouse in the corner, you would see that the participants actually start to live their roles. The roles and the case itself, become very real to them. Enthusiasm keeps building. Ideas are stimulated. The teacher (chairperson of the meeting) asks piercing questions of individuals. Consensus begins to develop. They are deeply into the "thinker-debater" trance.

If you want to see it in action, you can get videos from Harvard or almost any university library.

Once you become adept at using the strange language of

hypnosis, you will find that it sort of automatically works itself into you language as you speak to classes, or to anyone else. You will find words like "imagine", "picture", "wonder", "discover", and sentences ending in question marks, creeping into your choice of words.

Telling stories, (or "building scenarios" in academia-ese) can be used to create a hypnotic mood in class. Take them somewhere that is not here and now. The art of story-telling is the art of hypnosis. Watch "Mr. Rogers Neighborhood." Once the mood is created, you can take them wherever you want them to go.

Someone asked in one of my hypnosis workshops; "Is hypnosis a form of learning, or is learning a form of hypnosis?"

My own suggestion would be that learning without some element of trance is merely rote memorizing.

Romance

If you have ever seen the movie "Shenandoah" With Jimmy Stewart, you may remember the scene where he is talking to a young army officer, who is

courting his daughter. Jimmy asks:

"Do you like her?"

"I <u>love</u> her!"

"No. No- I mean do you <u>like</u> her?"

Myself, as an old therapist who has seen a great many relationships at an intimate and pervasive perspective; I think there is a lot of wisdom in asking that question.

I have a friend who is a retired bar owner and entertainer, who had been married a number of times. Once, in a pensive mood, she said to me:

"Walt, I've gotten myself married for a number of reasons. I've married for love. I've married for sex. I've married for money, and I've married for status. I've married because everyone else was doing it. Next time I'm going to marry someone who's polite."

And that's pretty much all I have to say about the whole matter. If you want a lasting relationship, start with a real friendship and let it build from there. It naturally will. If love comes before friendship, the friendship is not likely to ever come. And love without friendship is like a fish on a bicycle. Don't run your heart too fast, because it can get you into a wide variety of deep trouble. As the old German saying goes: "Kissin' don't last. Cookin' do."

How do you get someone to like you?" Recall the "Golden

Secret" that we talked about earlier? You simply like them first. They are very likely to return the favor.

"Active Listening", which we discussed, is very, very endearing. Ask them about themselves, get them to explain themselves to you. Ask about their memories, first some good ones, then some bad ones. Tell them that they remind you of an old friend, and let them ask why. Ask if you, yourself remind them of someone. These are sharing's that are remembered.

We've come a long way, you and I. I wonder what will be the next step as you go about building yourself, as you dream about the future.

Appendix I

Choosing an Hypnotist/Hypnotherapist

You should be aware that hypnosis is a largely unregulated service., except as overseen by health insurers. In the United States, only three States require registration of hypnotists and hypnotherapists, and only one of those requires an exam. Six States have issued guidelines for practice (mostly specifying what should not be done), but do not require registration. No State requires licensure. All of the other States do not have specific regulations concerning hypnosis.

But don't let that concern you. This means that Legislatures recognize that hypnosis is no more and no less dangerous than any other human interaction. Also, how could hypnosis be defined, so that it could be separated from any other type of structured persuasion, such as parenting or supervision or marketing? Hypnotists buy about as much malpractice insurance as sales managers do. (none) The only risk is if the hypnotist does something deliberately malicious or dangerous, and that is not malpractice, it's just plain general liability.

As for the rest of the world, it seems that governments have concluded that it is just none of their business.

A fundamental fact about hypnosis is; success and failure are so very obvious. Either it works or it doesn't. That means that someone who is not competent will just disappear, because hypnotherapists live and die on referrals. It is very unlikely that someone who isn't competent would even try to offer hypnosis. Nevertheless, I suggest that you avoid places like tattoo parlors that also have an hypnosis room in the back. But you knew that.

Here's some simple guidelines:

1. Ask around. Friends, physicians, clergy etc. are likely to have heard about someone who does good work. Most dentists, nurses, physical therapists, and social workers know someone. Reputation is everything.

2. If they have had a presentable office, a receptionist, and a yellow pages listing for some time, they're probably good. One cannot make a living in the field unless they are good. A neighborhood office implies that they have a lot of repeat and referral clients.

3. An advanced degree is a good sign. Yet I have known some very good hypnotists without one. I think that an advanced degree in behavioral sciences is recommended for treatment of behavioral maladies, unless they have a really good reputation and track record.

4. I would much prefer to work in a multi- person practice. Hypnotists need to stimulate and inspire each other, so that they

don't get into a rut. Also, multiple practice means that they can match your presenting requests to someone who likes to specialize.

5. Ask your hypnotist about their qualifications. Ask about areas of special interest or special concentration. They don't mind that at all. You can make a few phone calls, if you want to verify. Beware of printed testimonials.

6. If, for any reason, you don't "click" with the person; move on. No hard feelings.

Appendix II

The Therapeutic Relationship.

Imagine, if you will, a place where you can express yourself, without the fear of contradiction or interruption. It is a quiet and comfortable place; a place where you are in control. You can speak at will, and you can ask for my responses to your words, if you wish. Nothing will ever leave this comfortable room. You can think out loud, and you can have time to ponder and reflect upon our own words. You can pause to think, and you don't need to talk faster, because you know you are being heard. You can explain your own self. And maybe you can learn more about your own self. How could that be bad? I'm thinking that you don't want any more advice, you need more of your own understanding.

I will ask difficult questions. (What did you do then? Did it work?)

Many of my new clients come in feeling some trepidation, about what happens here?

We have designed this place so that it can be entirely safe and private. It is your place.

If you want us to meet with your "significant others", we

will, but it will be for the purpose of looking for alternative ways of relating to each other. We look for ways toward success. I will often use the word-"imagine". It is such a glorious word, is it not?

Regarding the other thing- personal relationships. It is true that therapists and clients tend to fall in love. Natural.

But acting upon that love is illegal, and actionable. It is illegal before, after, and during therapy. If you meet your therapist at a social occasion, h/she will probably not speak to you unless you speak first. This is to protect your privacy. Don't get huffy. OK?

But there is more to that than merely a matter of law. It has to do with the nature of the therapeutic relationship itself. We found in the last chapter that when people find someone who actually, actively, and genuinely listen to them, they tend to love that person. They go into the "love" trance, and they talk themselves into probing their own souls; they reveal more of their deepest and secret thoughts and feelings than they ever had before, even to themselves! And in so doing, they discover answers, and they discover a more robust identity; which leads to a serenity. This is a very special relationship indeed!

When loved, the therapist feels a reciprocal urge to return that love. Natural. But there lies the horrendous danger. The therapeutic relationship is so encompassing that it leaves absolutely no room for any other kind of relationship. Other relationships carry too much baggage. We play games in other relationships. We strive for leadership, influence, admiration, and other advantages. We become deceptive and manipulative. We put on airs, and faces. We become different people, and become less than genuine.

When the therapeutic relationship becomes contaminated with a personal relationship (especially a sexual one), both relationship will be destroyed, often with cataclysmic personal; and emotional, consequences for both therapist and client. A great trust has been broken and thrown away. That is the reason it is illegal; and rightly so.

When the therapeutic relationship becomes contaminated with a personal relationship (especially a sexual one), both relationship will be destroyed, often with cataclysmic personal; and emotional, consequences for both therapist and client. A great trust has been broken and thrown away. That is the reason it is illegal; and rightly so.

256
Appendix III

A Bibliography, for those who like this topic.

If you would like to continue with hypnosis, I have compiled this list for suggested further reading. I would suggest that you begin with some of the classics, by Erickson, Rossi, Rosen, Zeig, Bandler, Gilligan, Gurgevich, O'Hanlon, Haley. Then if you like, go on to the latest works. But take your pick. (Notice how many have a colon -:- in the title. I don't know who started that. But hey! - Tradition!)

Actually, I suspect that you could better spend your time and money by going to actually experience hypnosis, at least once. Then, these words will better fall into place for you.

Aspromonte, Don. Green Light Selling: Your Secret Edge to Winning Sales and Avoiding Dead Ends. Metamorphous Pr, 1989.

Bandler, Richard. Patterns of Hypnotic Techniques of Milton H. Erickson. Grinder & Associates, 1997.

Bandler, Richard. Richard Bandler's Guide to Trance-formation: How to Harness the Power of Hypnosis to Ignite Effortless and Lasting Change. HCi, 2008.

Bandler, Richard and Grinder, John. Frogs Into Princes: Neuro Linguistic Programming. Real People Pr, 1979.

Bandler, Richard, and Grinder, John. The Structure of Magic: A Book About language and Therapy. Science and Behavior Books, 1971.

Banyan, Calvin D. Hypnosis and Hypnotherapy: Basic to Advanced Techniques for the Professional. Abbot Publishing House, 2001.

Battino, Rubin. Ericksonian Approaches: A Comprehensive Manual. Crown House Publishing, 2005.

Bryant, Mike and Mabbutt, Peter. Self Hypnosis for Dummies. For Dummies, 2010.

Elias, Jack. Finding True Magic: Transpersonal Hypnosis and Hypnotherapy/NLP. Five Wisdoms Press, 2005.

Gilligan, Stephen G. Therapeutic Trances:The Co-Operation Principle in Ericksonian Hypnotherapy. Routledge, 1986.

Gurgevich, Steven. Hypnosis House Call: A Complete Course in Mind-Body Healing. Sterling Ethos, 2011.

258

Haley, Jay. Uncommon Therapy: The Psychiatric Techniques of Milton H. Erickson, M.D. W.W. Norton & Company, 1993.

Hammond, Corydon D. Handbook of Hypnotic Suggestions and Metaphors. W.W. Norton & Company. 1990.

Hewitt, William W. Hypnosis for Beginners: Reach New Levels of Awareness & Achievement. Llewellen Publications, 2002.

Hunter, Roy C. The Art of Hypnosis: Mastering Basic Techniques.
Crown House Publishing, 2010.

Erickson, Milton H. Ericksonian Hypnosis: Applications, Preparation, and Research. (Monograph #5). Bruner/Mazel, 1989.

Erickson, Milton H. and Rosen, Sidney. My Voice Will Go With You" The Teaching Tales of Milton H. Erickson. W.W. Norton & Company, 1991.

Erickson, Milton H. and Rossi, Ernest Lawrence. Hypnotherapy: An Exploratory Casebook. Irvington Pub, 1980.

Erickson, Milton H. Life Reframing in Hypnosis

259

(Workshops and Lectures of Milton H. Erickson). Irvington Pub, 1984.

Erickson, Milton H., Rossi, Ernest L. and Rossi, Sheila I. Hypnotic Realities: The Induction of Clinical Hypnosis and Forms of Indirect Suggestion. Irvington Publishers 1976.

Ewin, Dabney. 101 Things I Wish I'd Known When I Started Hypnosis. Crown House Publishing, 2009.

Gurgevich, Steven. Relieve Anxiety with Medical Hypnosis. Sounds True, Incorporated, 2007.

Jones, Dan. Advanced Ericksonian Hypnotherapy Scripts: A Collection of Over 100 Hypnosis and Therapy Scripts. lulu.com, 2011.

Morgan, Dylan. Hypnosis for Beginners. Laurier Books, Ltd., 2002.

Norgard, Richard. Keys to the Mind: Learn How to Hypnotize Anyone and Practice Hypnosis and Hypnotherapy Correctly. Peach Tree Professional Education, Inc., 2009.

O'Briain, Cathal. Powerful Mind Through Self Hypnosis: A Practical Guide to Complete Self-Mastery. O-Books. 2010.

260
O'Hanlon, William Hudson. A Guide to Trance Land: A Practical Handbook of Ericksonian and Solution Oriented Hypnosis. W.W. Norton & Company, 2009.

Nash, Mike and Barnier, Amand. The Oxford Handbook 0f Hypnosis: Theory, Research, and Practice. Oxford University Press, USA. 2012.

Pincus, David; Sheikh, A. and Rossi, Ernest L. Imagery for Pain Relief: A Scientifically Grounded Guidebook. T&F Books, US. 2011.

Powers, Melvin. A Practical Guide to Self-Hypnosis. Fili-Quarian Classics, 2010.

Rogers, Carl. Client Centered Therapy. The Riverside Press. 1951

Rossi, Ernest Lawrence. Mind-Body Therapy: Methods of Idiodynamic Healing in Hypnosis. W.W. Norton & Company, 1994.

Rossi, Ernest Lawrence. Psychobiology of Mind-Body Healing: New Concepts of Therapeutic Hypnosis. W.W. Norton & Company, 1993.

261

Simpkins, Alexander. Neuro-Hypnosis: Using Self Hypnosis to Activate the Brain for Change. Norton Professional Books, 2010.

Sommer, Carol. Conversational Hypnosis: A Manual of Indirect Suggestion. Sommer Solutions, Inc., 1992.

Starr, Jo Ana. Quantum Self Hypnosis: Awaken the Genius Within. CreateSpace, 2011.

Stevenson, Michael. Learn Hypnosis...Now!. Liquid Mirror Enterprises, 2004.

Temes, Roberta. The Complete Idiot's Guide to Hypnosis, (2nd LOL). Alpha, 2004.

Weil, Andrew and Gurgevich, Steven. Heal Yourself with Medical Hypnosis: The Most Immediate Way to Use Your Mind-Body Connection. Sounds True, Incorporated, 2005.

Yapko, Michael D. Mindfulness and Hypnosis: The Power of Suggestion to Transform Experience. W.W. Norton & Company, 2011.

Zeig, Jeffrey K. Ericksonian Approaches to Hypnosis and Psychotherapy. Bruner/Mazel, 1989.

PORTLAND PUBLIC LIBRARY SYSTEM
5 MONUMENT SQUARE
PORTLAND, ME 04101

05/22/2014 $18.95

Made in the USA
Charleston, SC
16 May 2014